HILHAVEN LODGE

HILHAVEN LODGE
The Photo Booth Pictures

Photo Strips by Brett Ratner
Introduction by Robert Evans

pH powerHouse Books New York, NY

Hilhaven Lodge was designed by architect Gordon Kaufman in 1927 as the guesthouse to Hilhaven, which was the main residence (no longer in existence), constructed in 1923. The original owner of the estate was Charles B. Hopper and family. Hilhaven Lodge was sold to Ingrid Bergman during World War II, and then sold to Kim Novak and Richard H. Quine in the 60s. It was later sold to Allan Carr in 1972, and finally to Brett Ratner in 2000.

Whether it be a Monet watercolor, a Frank Lloyd Wright home, a Henry Moore sculpture, or a Michael Jordan jump shot, they all share one commonality. No price too high does an original bear. That too fits Brett Ratner.

Why? Forgetting his talent, which is extraordinary, he is only one of three I have known who has proved to be the real thing, "a Kid." The other two being Walt Disney and Michael Eisner. Don't underestimate the power of a Kid. He can read an adult's mind far better than an adult can read his. He discerns truth from falsehood without ever showing his hand. He is devoid of cynicism, and he gives of himself without seeking reciprocity. Having the mind of a Kid in an adult's world brings to the table the unknown. The power of the unknown, when used properly, can be historic.

I met Walt Disney when I was a kid. Years later, I uncovered his genius. He too was a Kid. Whatever film he produced, he allowed only one person to sit with him and watch the dailies of the previous day's work. It was not the head of distribution or the head of production; it was a twelve-year-old boy. An actor under contract to the studio by the name of Kurt Russell. Young Kurt's advice as to what he had just seen had an unbiased purity that Walt appreciated and responded to most. One Kid trusting another kid's opinion, far more than he would any adult's.

Decades later, I was on the tennis court when my butler interrupted the match.
    "Michael Eisner is at the door wanting to speak with you."
    Was my butler crazy? Just the morning before, Eisner had been named the new head of Paramount, and he's ringing my doorbell? Dropping my racket, I made it to the door quick. Standing before me was a tall young man looking as though he had just graduated college.
    Before I had a chance to congratulate him on his new appointment, he put out his hand.
    "It's an honor, Mr. Evans, to meet you."
    Naturally, I invited him in. Walking through my gardens, I'm thinking to myself, "This is the new president of Paramount?" I offered him a drink, a bite of lunch.
    "Oh, no thank you, sir. I did come here though to ask a favor. It's something very important to me, and I'd appreciate it if it didn't go past the two of us."
    "No problem, sit down."
    "Mr. Evans, I need your help."
    "Sure, what is it?"
    "I've done very well in the world of television, maybe too well."
    Then, bending over to me, half-whispering, "I don't know how to say this, but I don't know anything about making movies, and I hope I don't sound too aggressive to you, but I don't want to fail. What I am trying to say is, I need your help. Teach me. At least teach me what not to do."

Disarming? No, brilliant. These words could only come from the genuineness of a Kid in distress. I did help him out. Big. For more than a year, he looked up to me as his model. Well, the student sure in hell one upped his model.

It was a year later. Me? I was desperate to make a film on tennis. Michael turned me down cold.
    "You taught me too well Evans, there's never been an audience for a picture about tennis."
    Getting an Eisner "no" got my head tickin'. How do you get to a Kid? Make him a dare.
    A week later, while lunching at the Paramount commissary together, I threw him a curve.
    "You know, Michael, for more than a hundred years, Wimbledon has never opened its gates to anyone. They are English conservative to the hilt. 'No Exploitation' is their model. Do I know it? They wouldn't let me in without a tie on. What if I get them snobs to open their gates and let me shoot the picture with their full cooperation. Then will you give me the green light?"
    So loud, his laughter, that everyone at the tables surrounding us had turned to see what was so funny.
    "You're getting Wimbledon to let you shoot a picture there? Are you crazy?"
    "Yeah. But it's a dare I can't refuse."
    "What's the budget?"
    "About six mil."
    "If you get Wimbledon, forget six, I'll give you seven!"
    Tears of laughter ran down his face as I grabbed for a napkin and scribbled down the details of his impromptu promise. Pushing it in front of him, I staccatoed, "Sign it." He quickly did.

"Why did you ask me to sign it?"

"Michael, remember? One of the first things I taught you was if it ain't signed, it ain't collectible."

With childlike laughter, he shook his head.

"You're right. You're right."

Well, I got Wimbledon. And Michael...got Disney. The picture? A total flop.

Disney? Well, let's just say that it was the Kid in Eisner that turned an all but dead Mickey Mouse into the Hope Diamond. There has only been one other Kid I have ever encountered these decades past. His name? Brett Ratner.

Truthfully, I was somewhat suspect of his childlike enthusiasm upon first meeting him. His mind, mouth, and ambitions moved faster than a Maserati on the autobahn. In times past, I had met all too many fast-talking, enthusiastic characters who proved to be all talk and no thought not to think that, "This kid's either P.T. Barnum or the biggest bullshitter I'd ever met."

Days turned to weeks, weeks to months, and months to years. How extraordinary, I realized that this Ratner is the real thing. I've met a third Kid.

Of the three, he is by far the most giving of himself, his time, his energy, and his genuine desire to help others in their climb up a very steep ladder. Both professionally and personally, his giving is a one-way street. Reciprocity never enters the equation. His success may come from his talent, but there are many talented people. Ahh, but his persona, singular.

Truth's truth, this totally original book of photos proves my point best. Here is an artist whose films have grossed into the stratosphere, whose dance card is filled for years to come to maestro most anything he wishes. Yeah, but that isn't as important to him as taking the many friends he has embraced at his home into a simple photo booth, no more sophisticated than one you would see at an arcade, and snapping strips of pictures. No lighting, no makeup, no airbrush, just a photographic remembrance of time spent together. It is the only book of photography I have ever seen that captures personas—especially of Hollywood personalities—this candidly.

Brett looks upon this collection of images as a labor of love, giving it the same care and passion as he would any major film production. While rolls of quarters were its budget, rolls of millions couldn't have bought its cast. They did it for Brett, and Brett did it for us. His simple "Photo Booth" has captured the magic of the still frame in its most raw form. Like its creator, it is a one of a kind, totally devoid of pretense. Only a Kid could have pulled it off.

Robert Evans, 2003

A blinking light, a sudden flash, a minute wait and there they were...four funny faces before my eyes. Can't deny it—it was love at first sight. And it's only gotten better.

My first purchase upon buying Hilhaven Lodge in 2000 was not a bed, a table, or a refrigerator. It was a third-hand photo booth. Best buy I've ever made. No wealth could have afforded me the meaningful moments, ebullience, and instant gratification than that of a simple, beaten-up, magical booth.

Brett Ratner, 2003

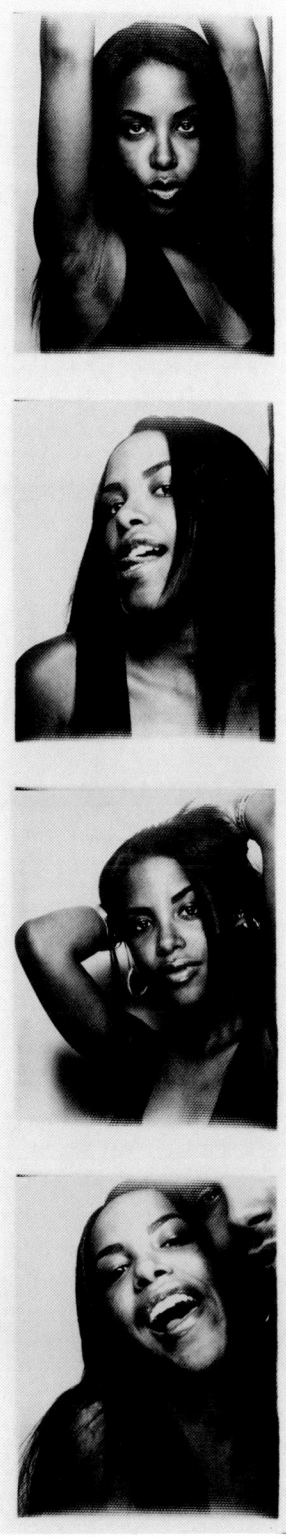

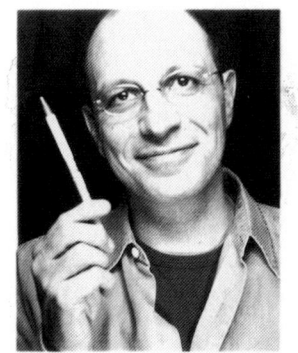
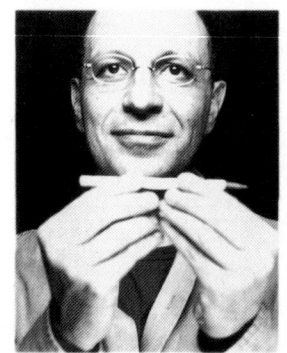
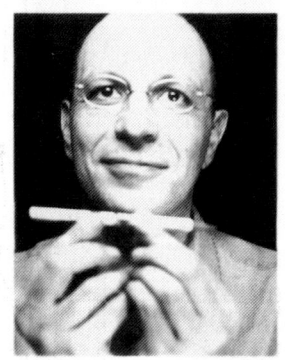
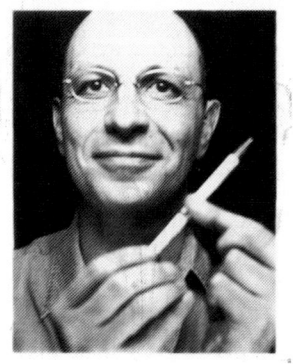

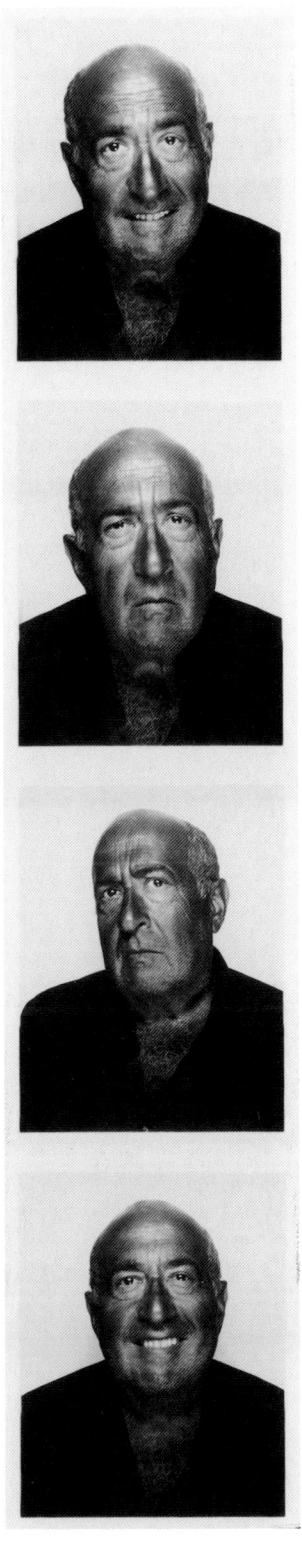

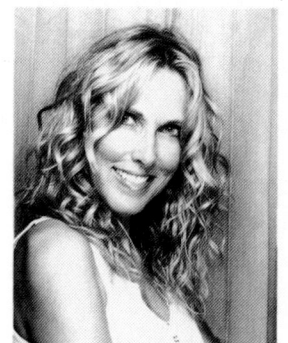

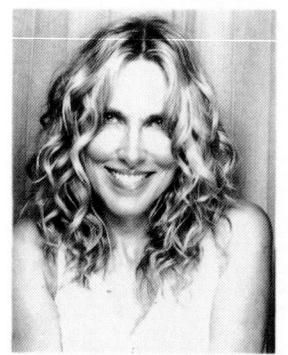

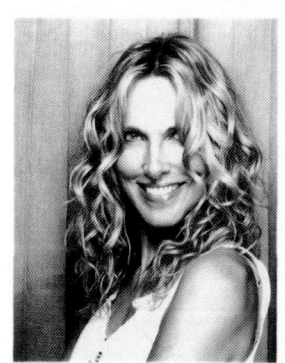

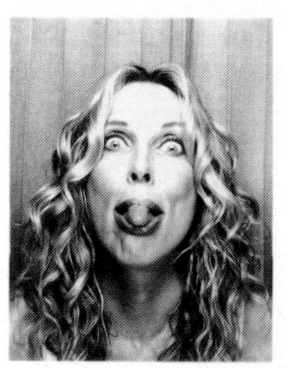

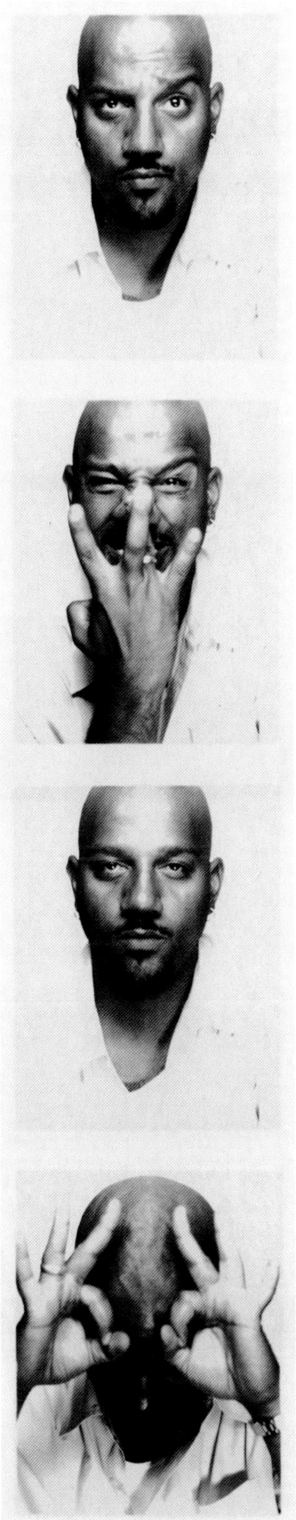

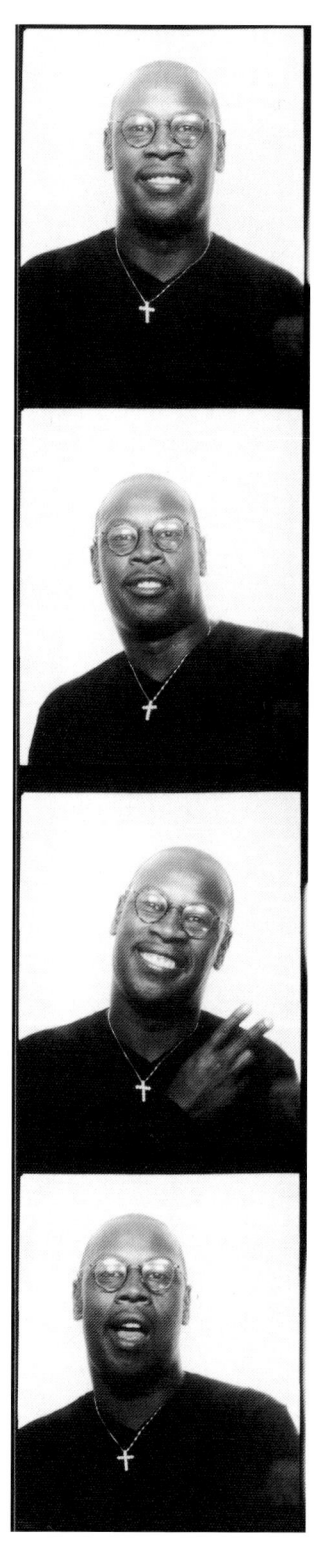

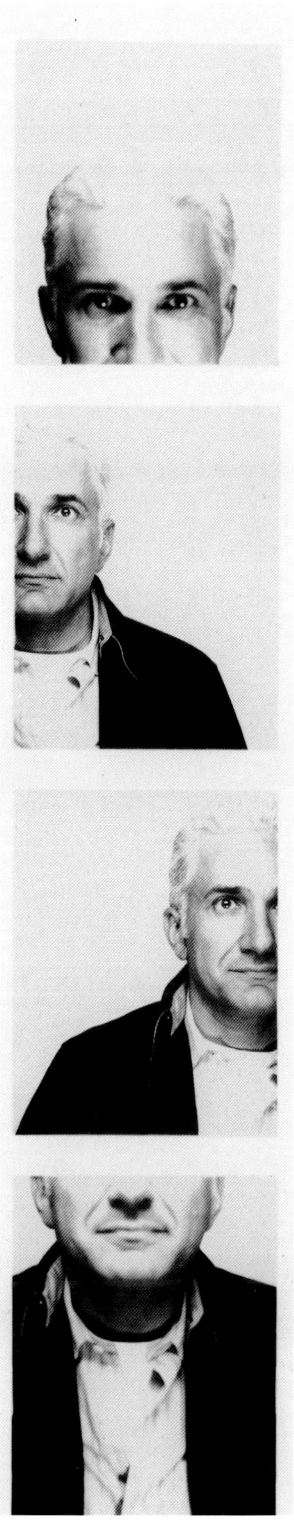

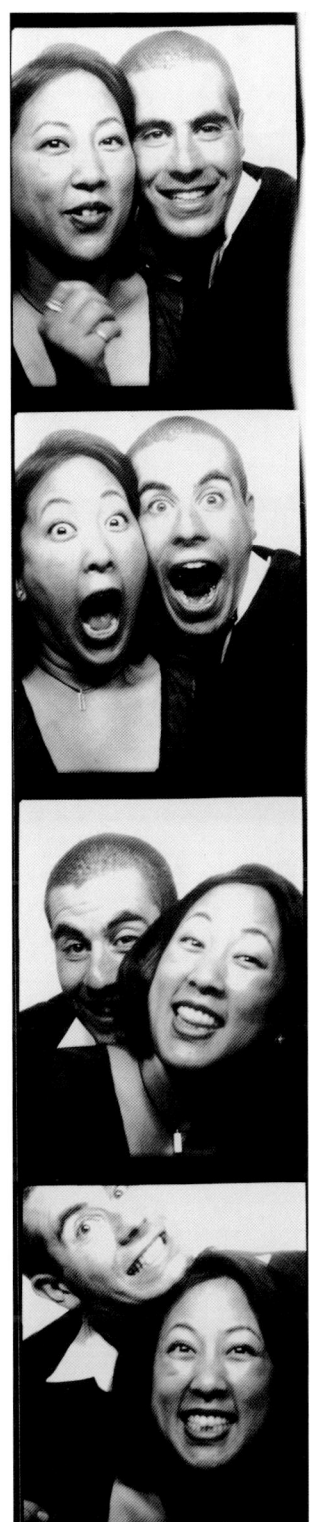

Anita S. Chang & David Steiman

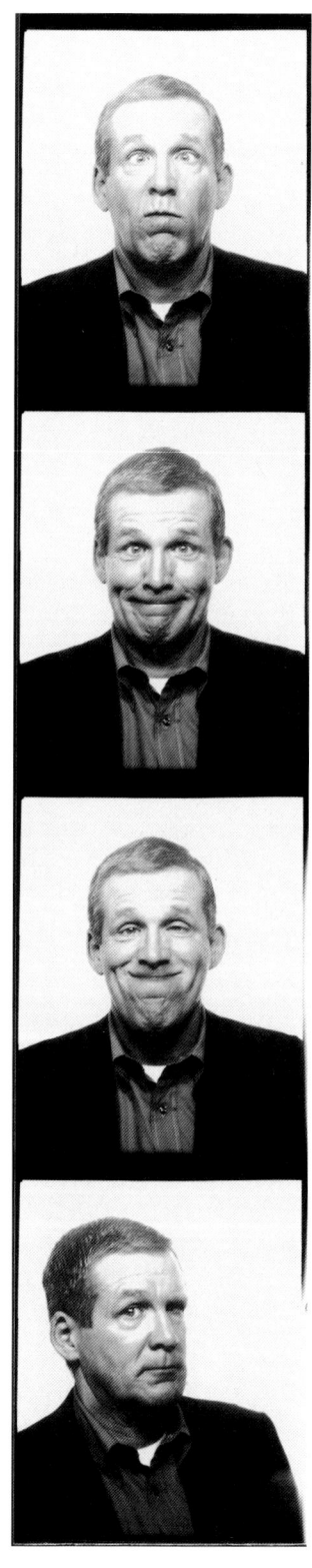

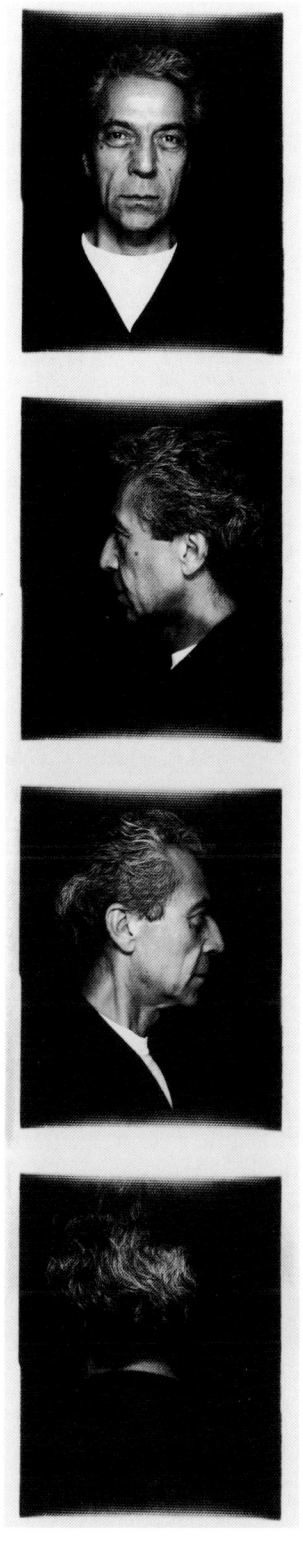

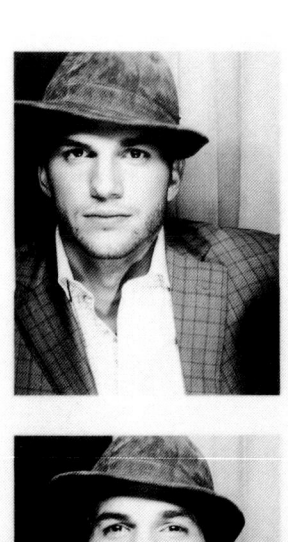
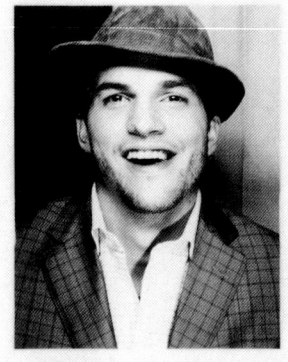
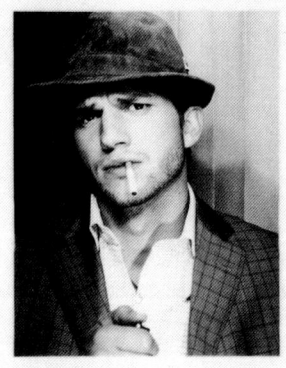
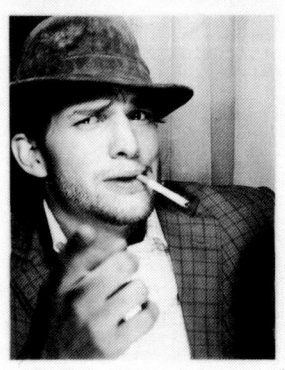

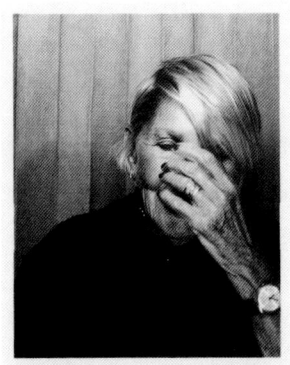

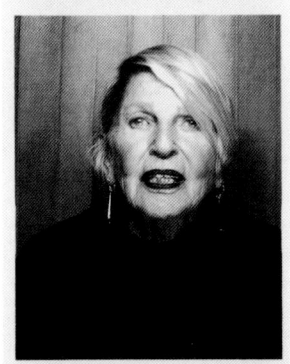

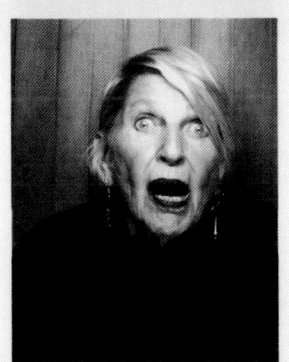

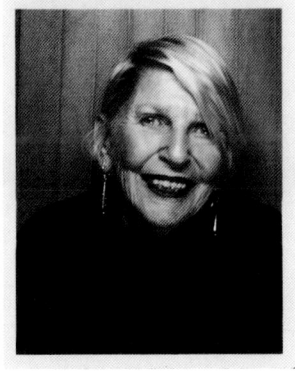

Bea Milwe

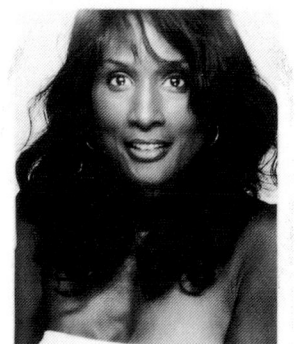
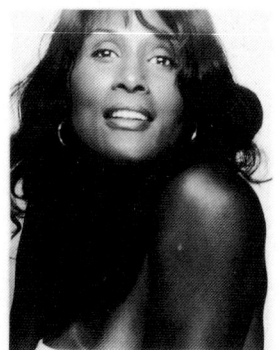
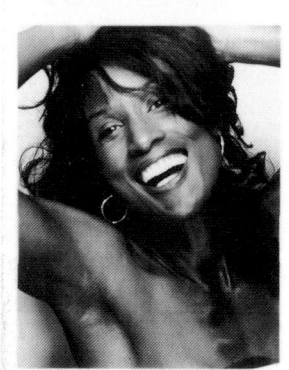
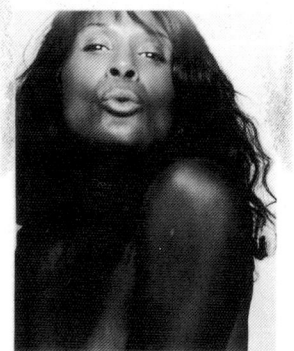

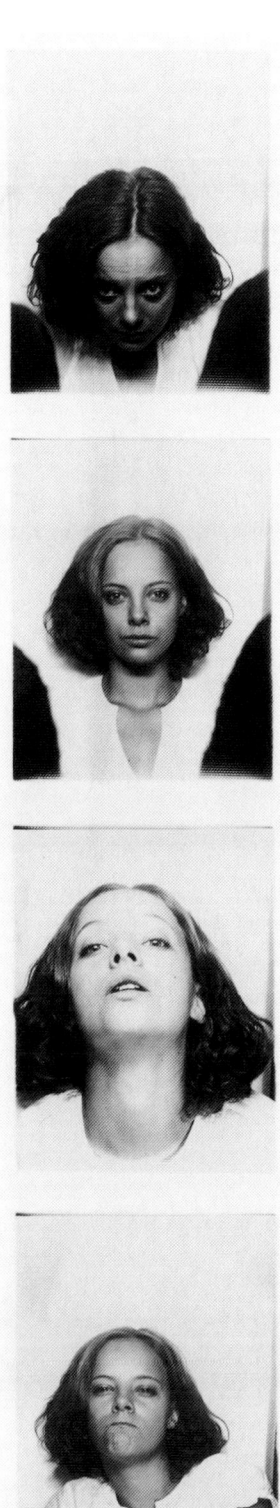

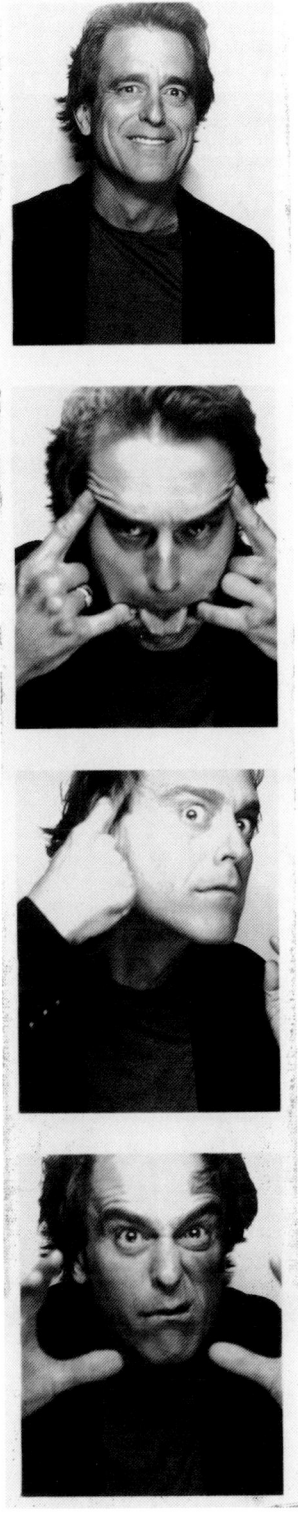

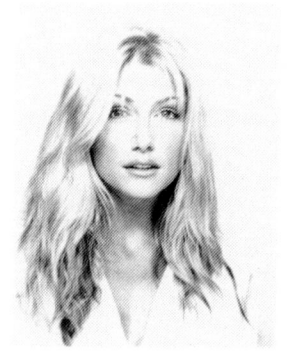

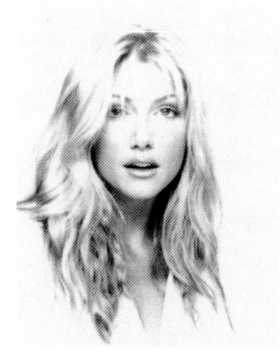

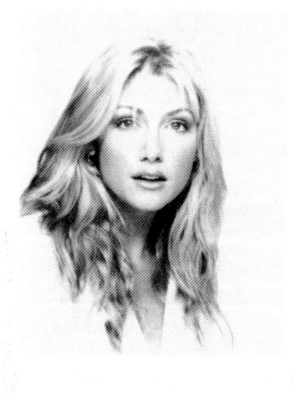

Brendan Fraser

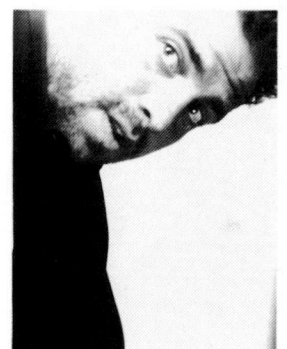

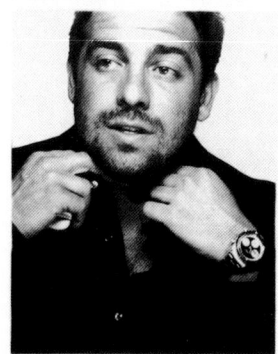

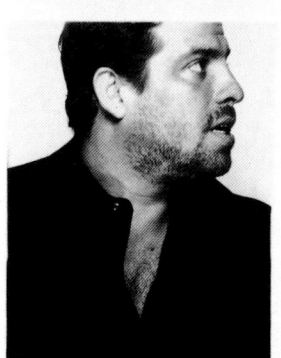

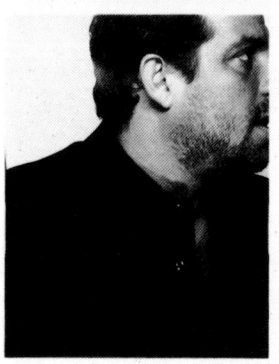

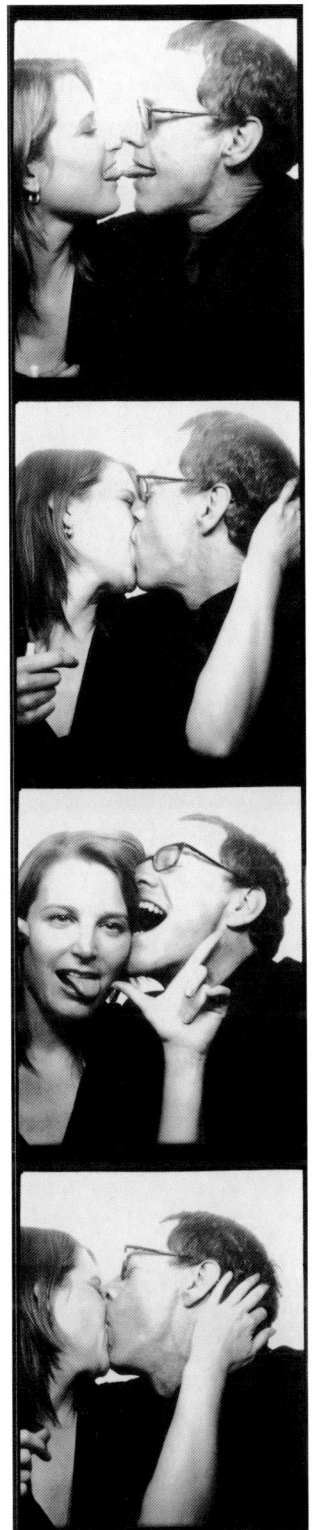

Bridget Fonda & Danny Elfman

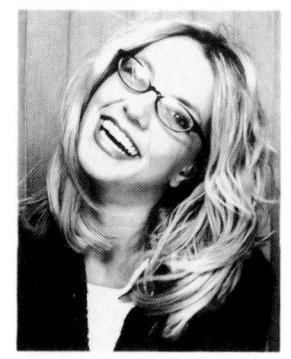

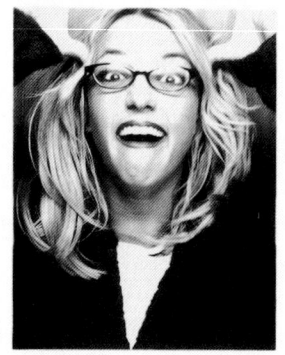

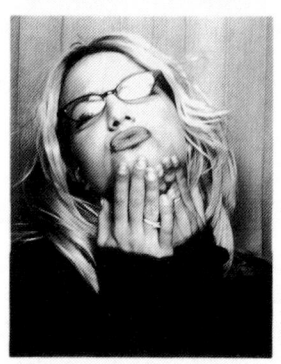

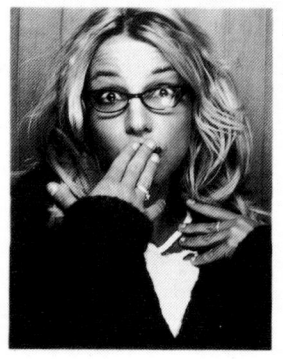

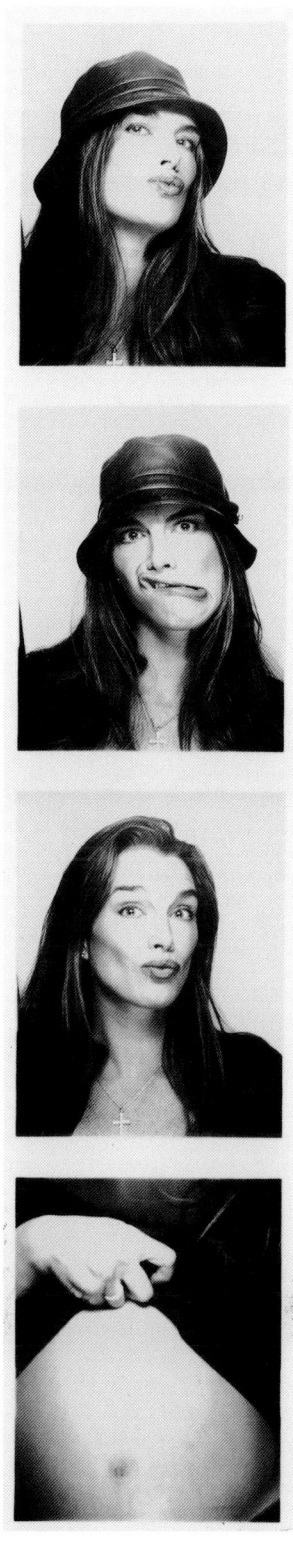

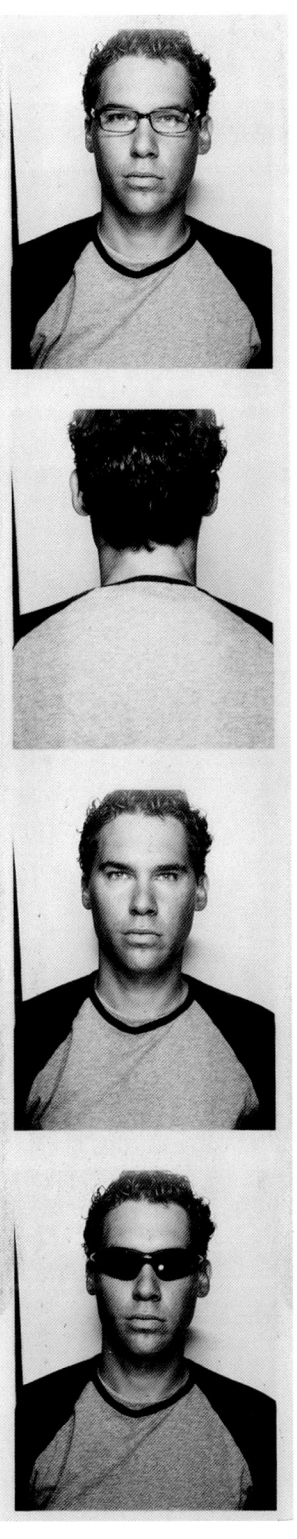

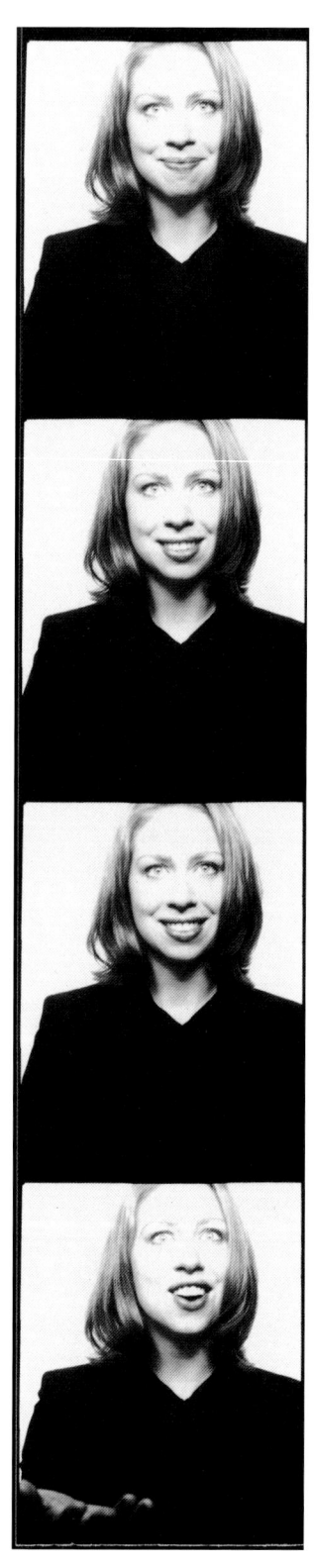

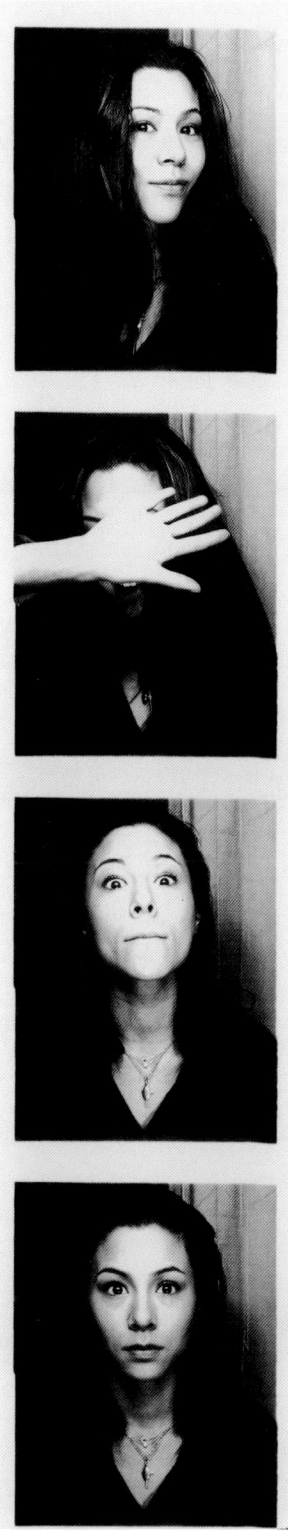

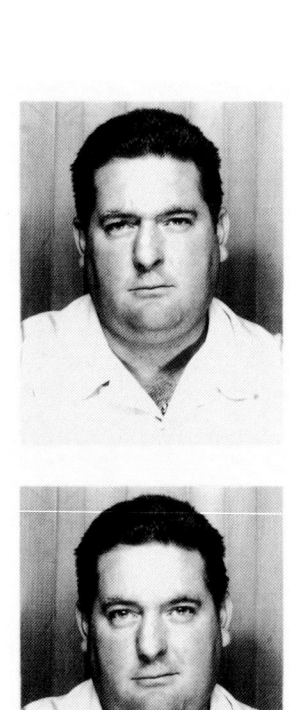
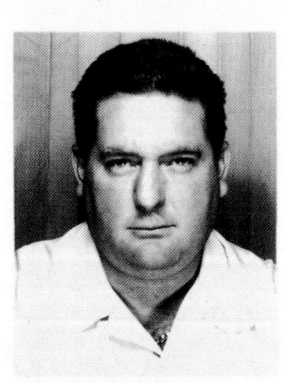
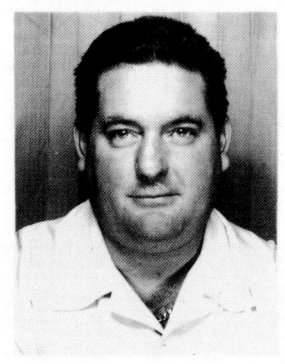

Chris Penn

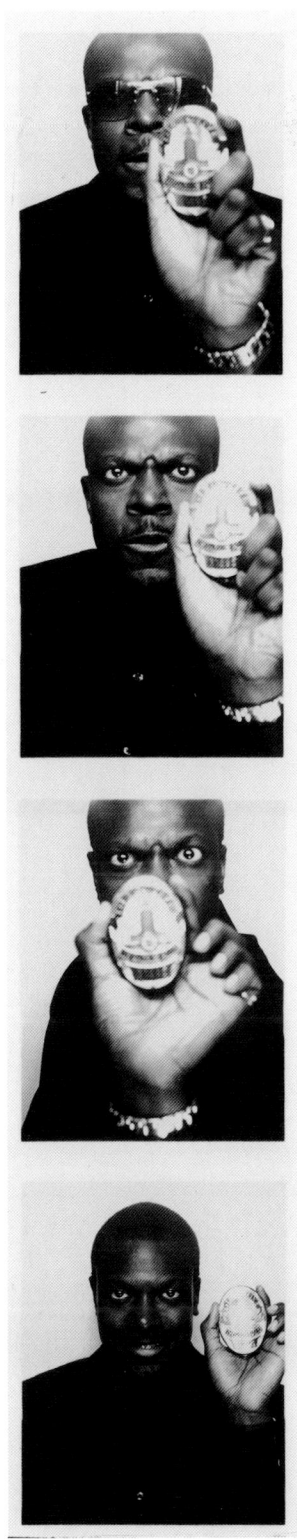

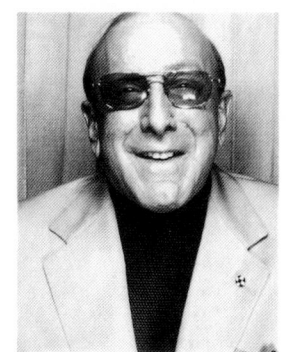
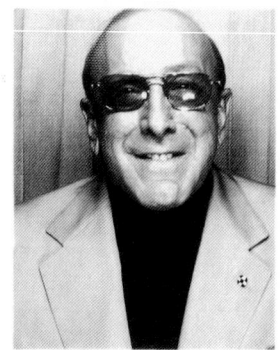
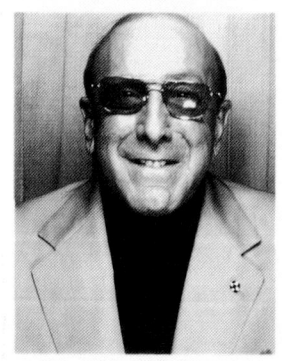
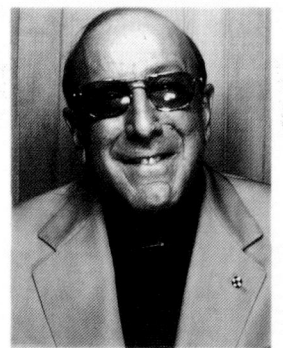

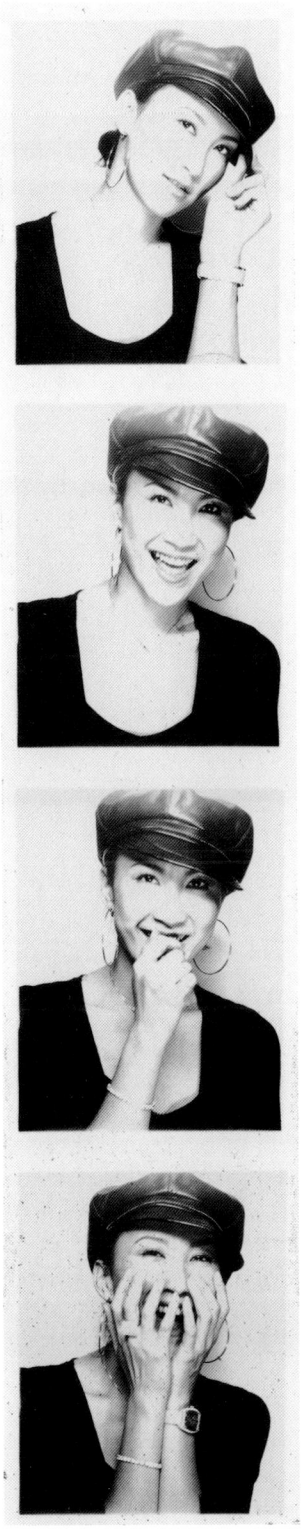

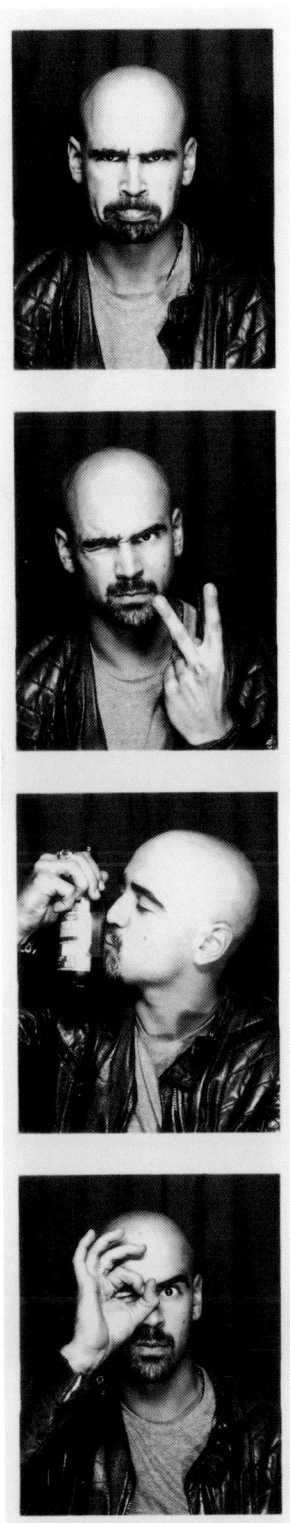

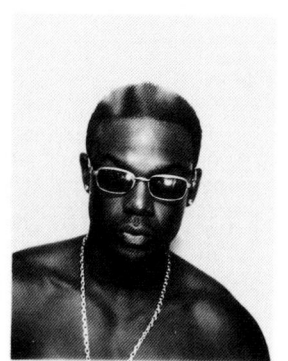

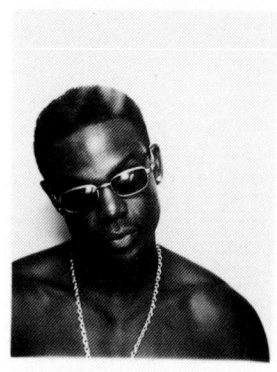

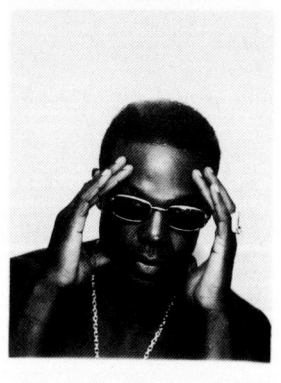

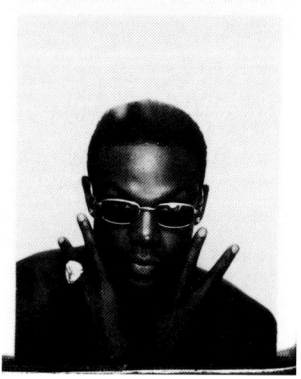

Dalvin DeGrate

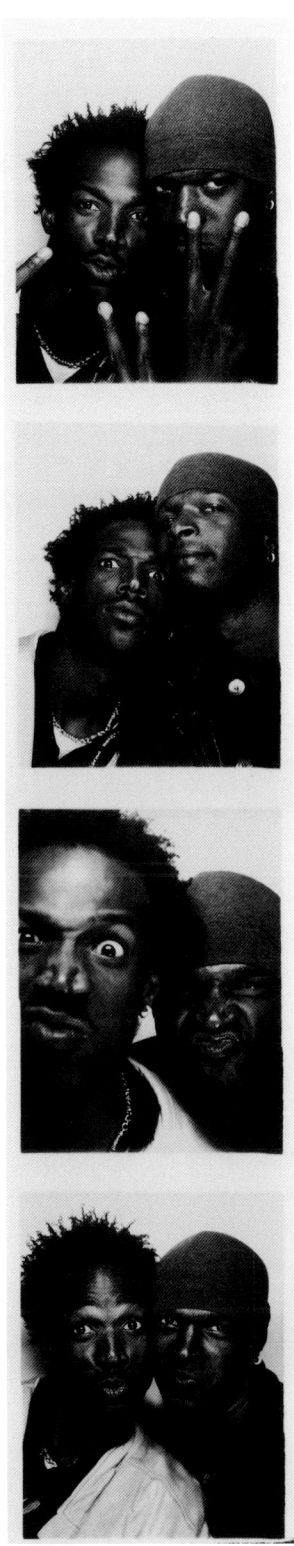

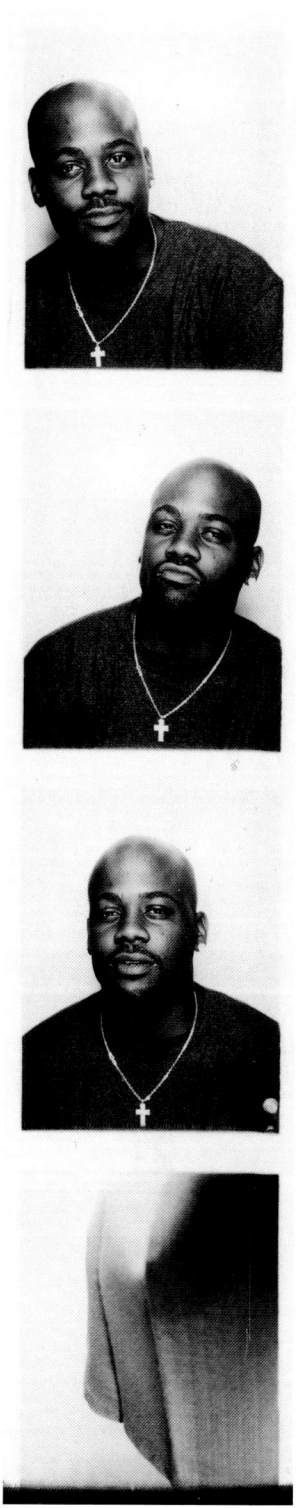

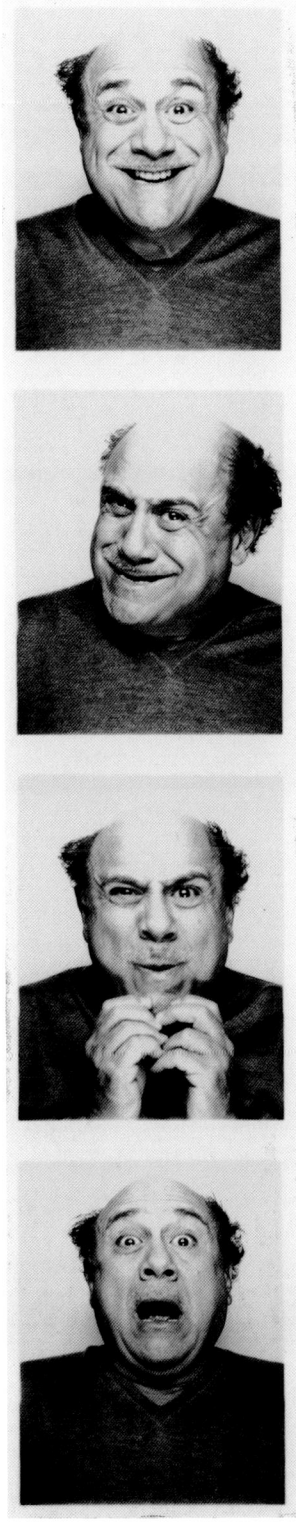

Danny DeVito

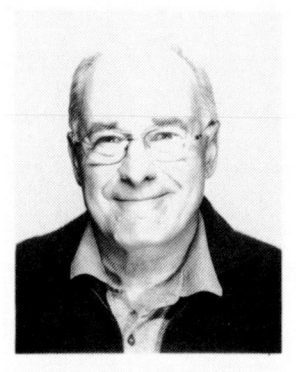
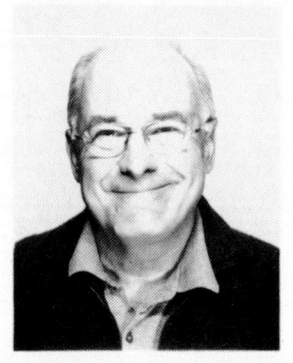
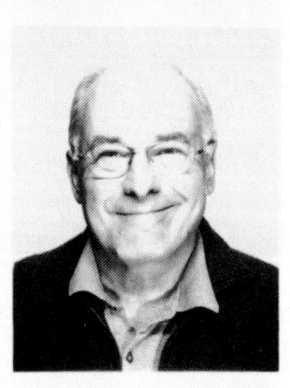
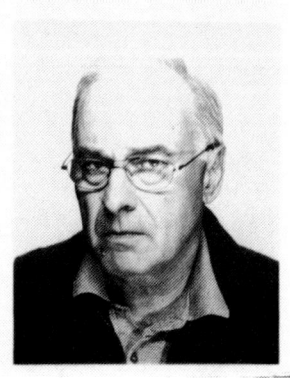

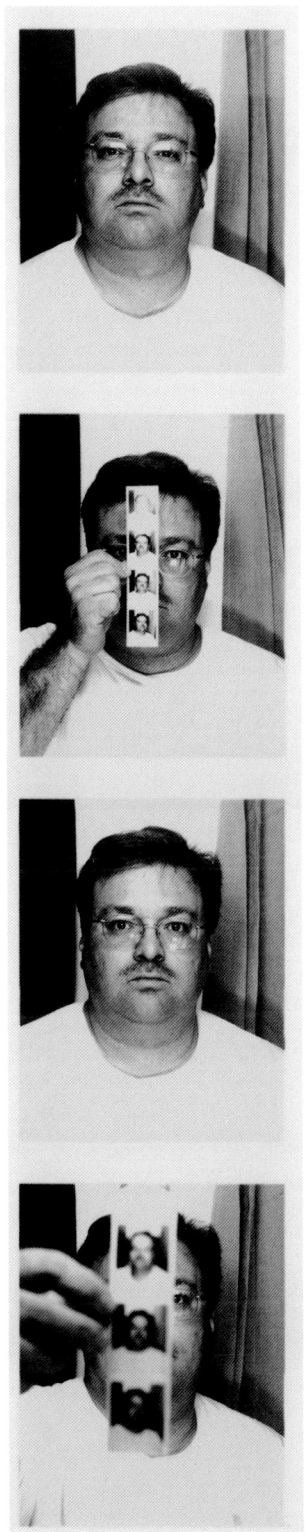

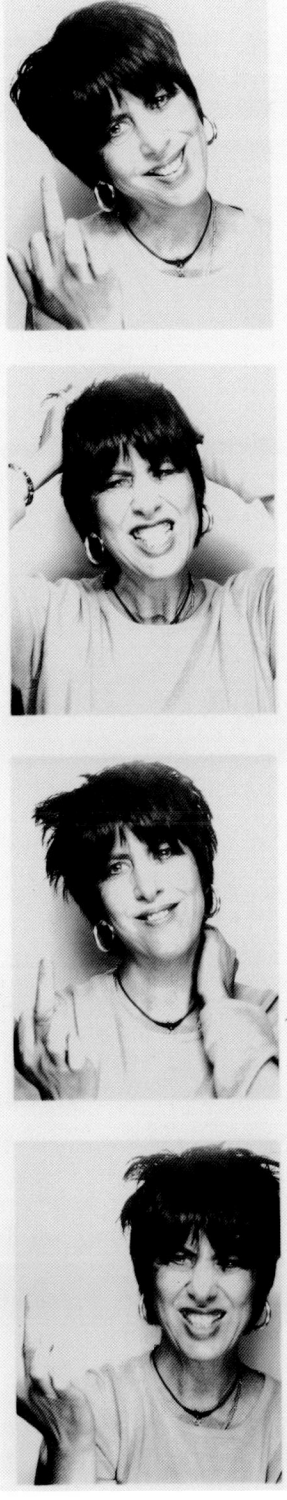

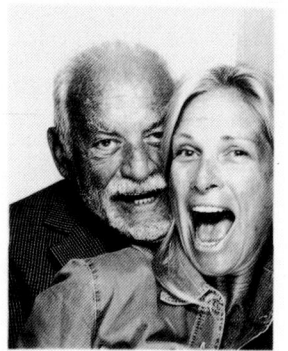

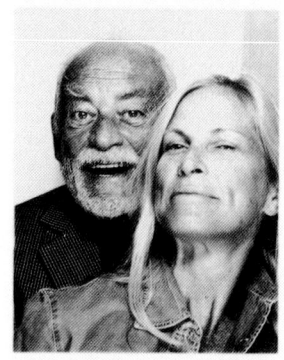

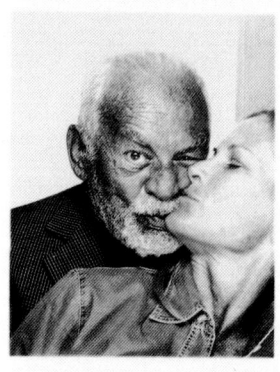

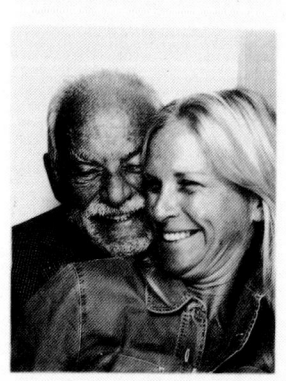

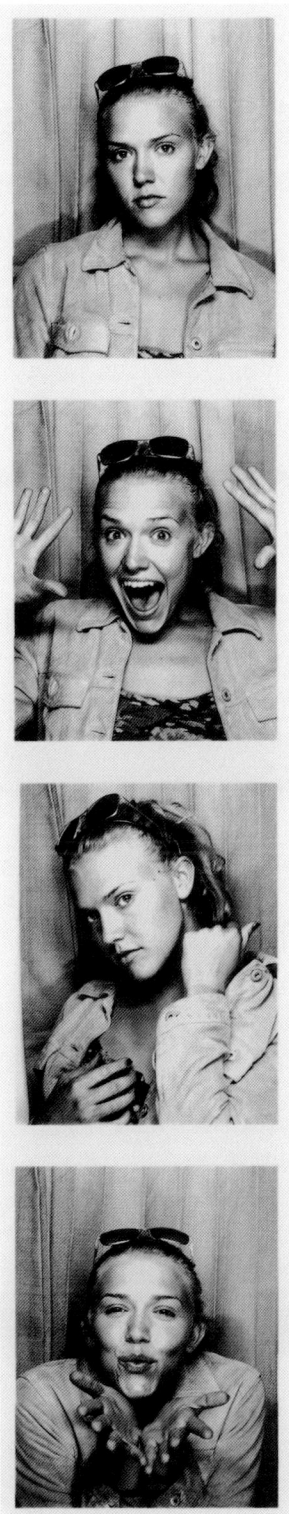

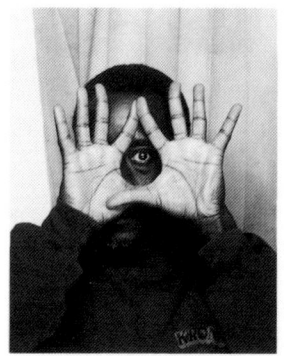

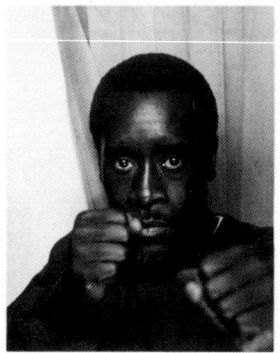

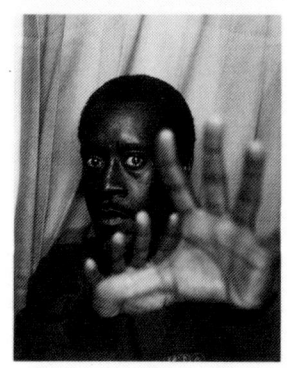

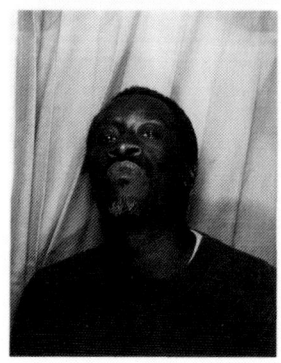

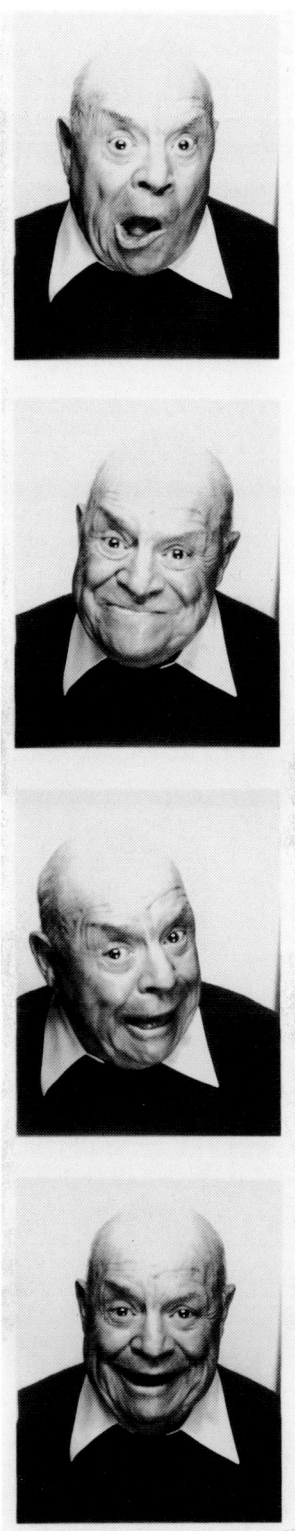

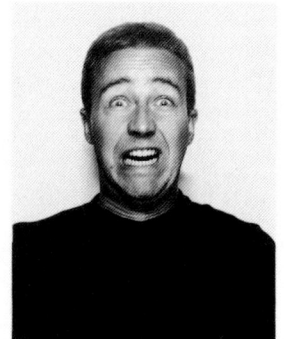
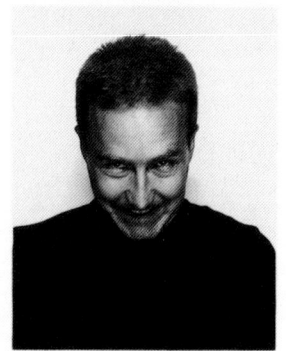
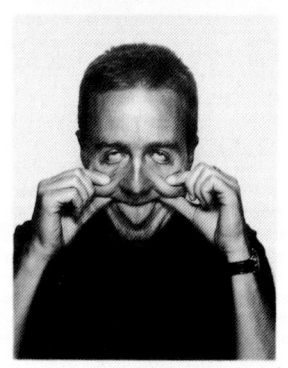
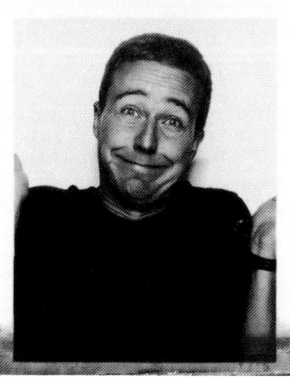

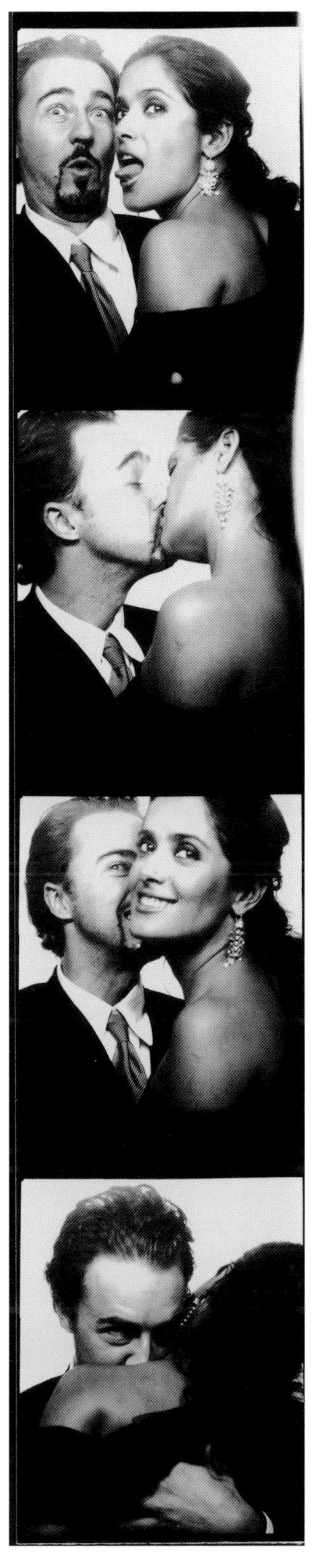

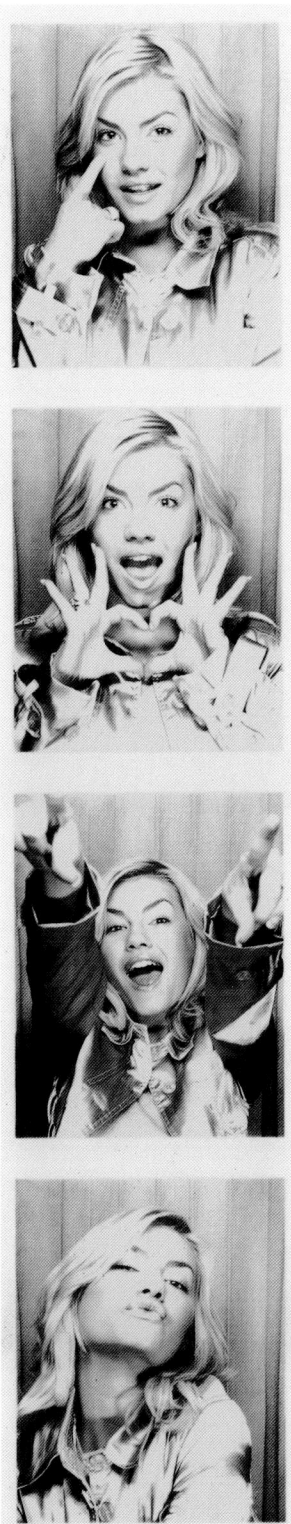

Elisha Cuthbert

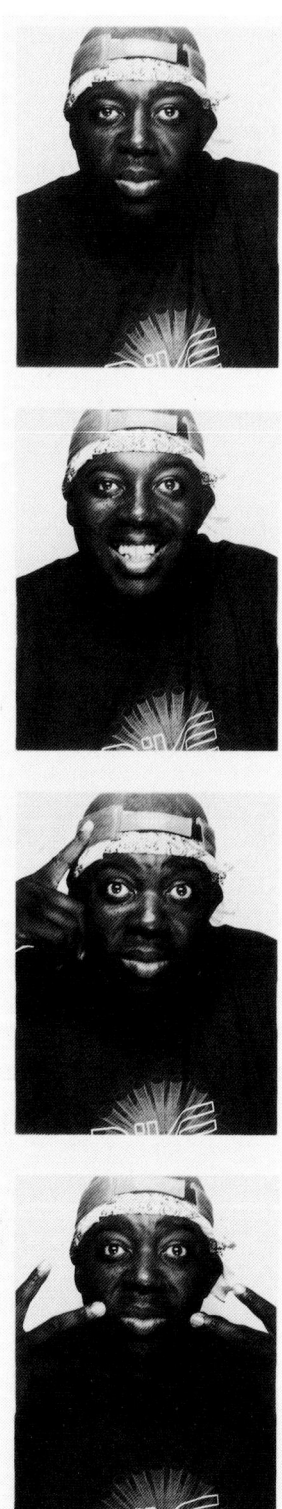

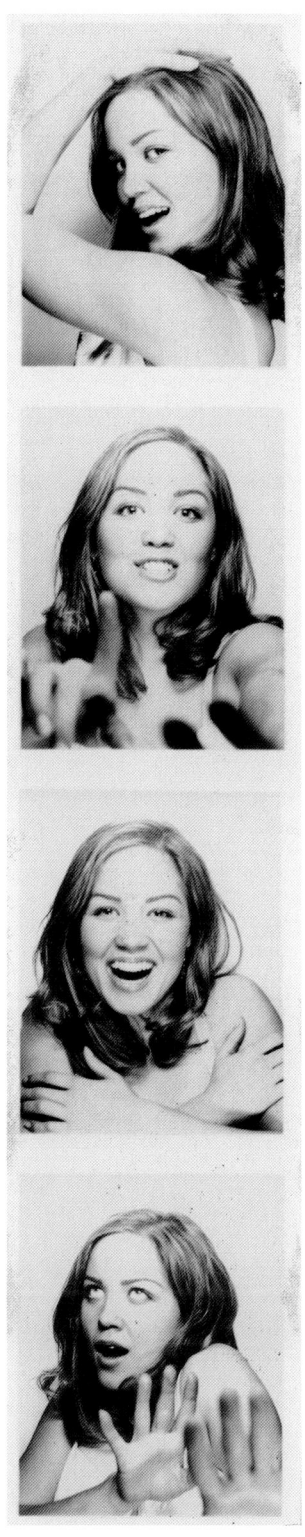

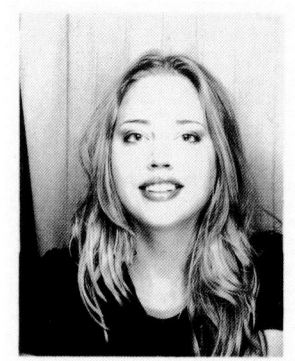
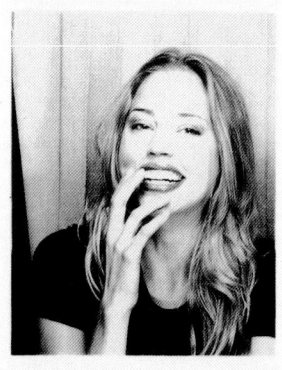
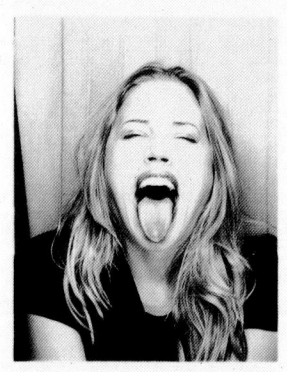
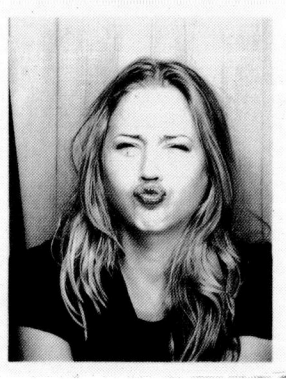

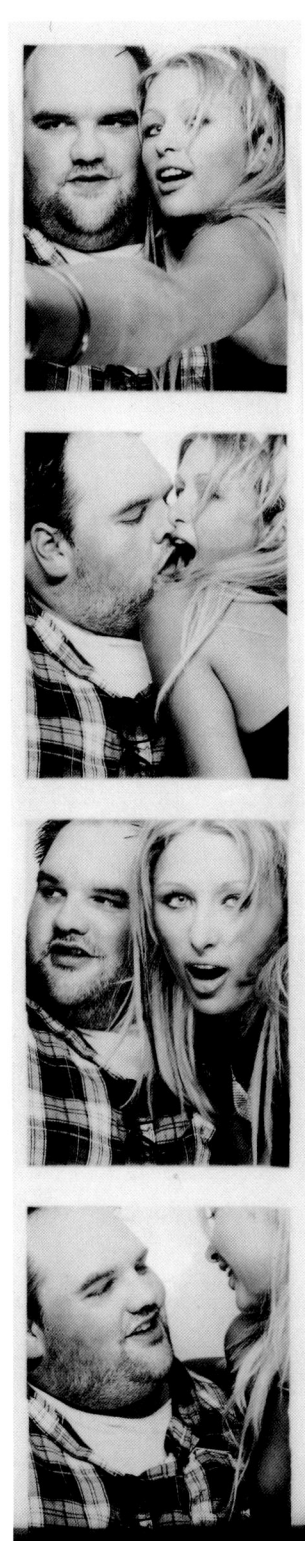

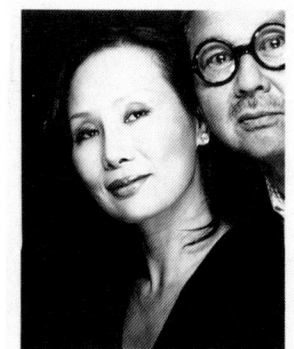
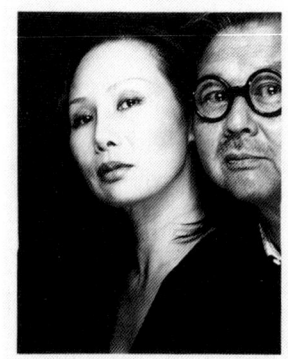
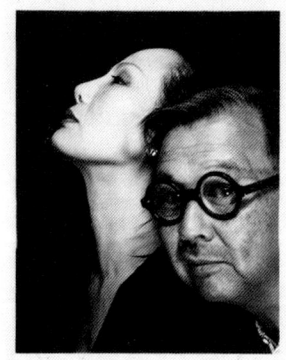
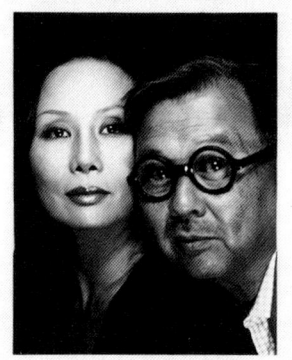

Eva & Michael Chow

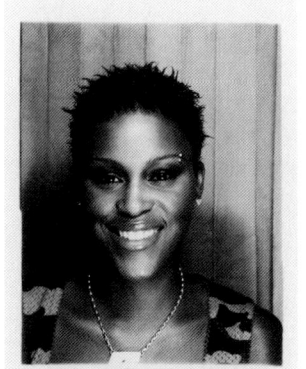
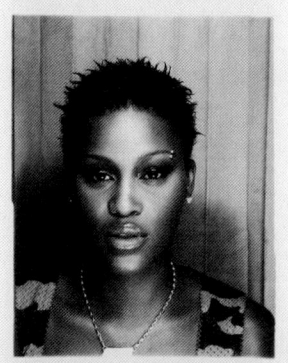
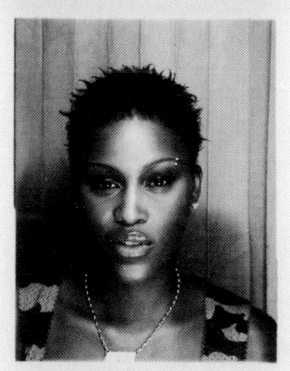
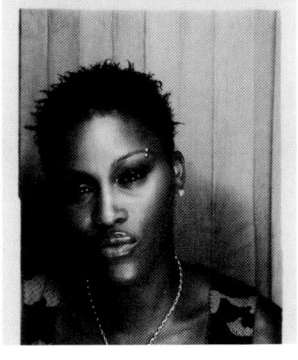

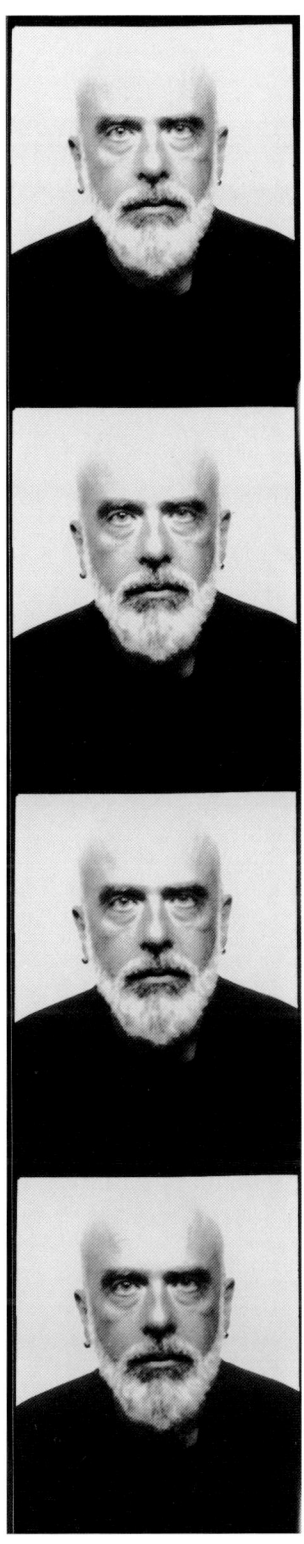

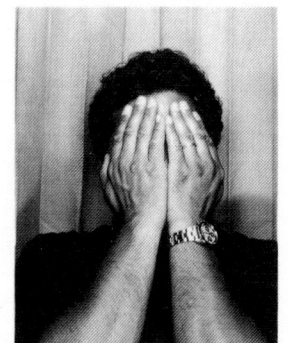
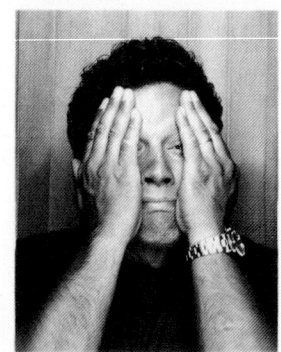
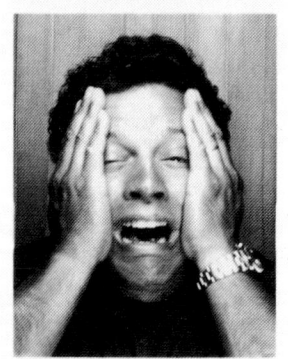
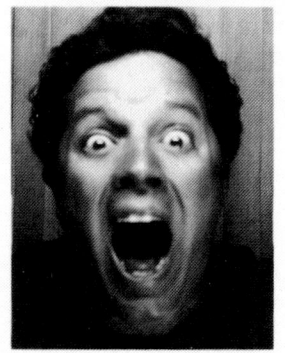

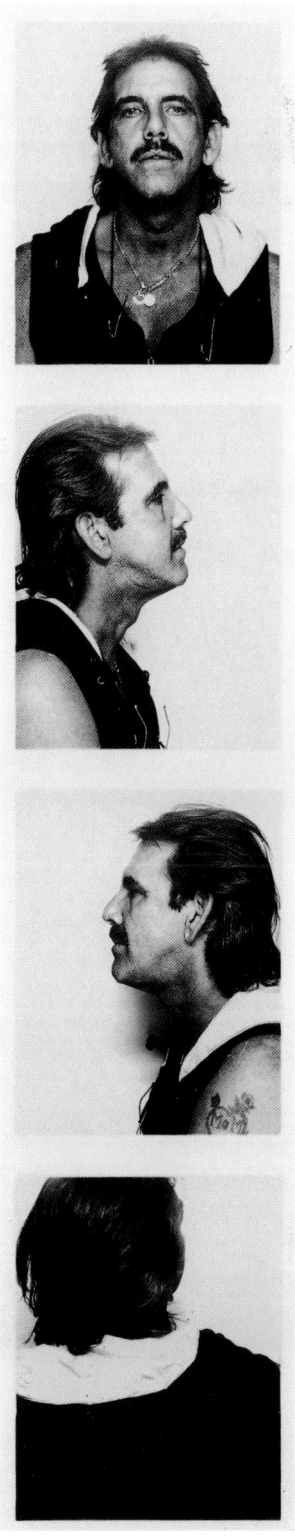

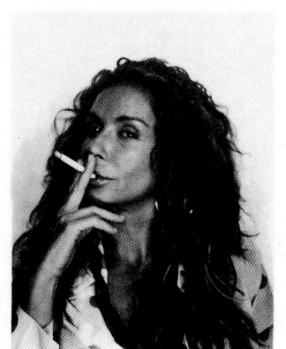

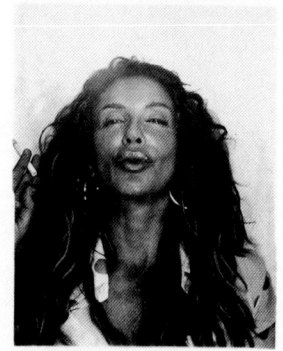

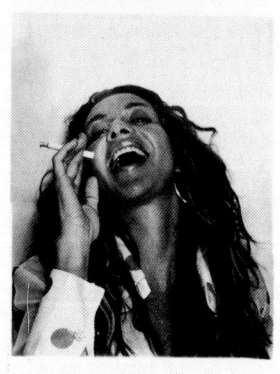

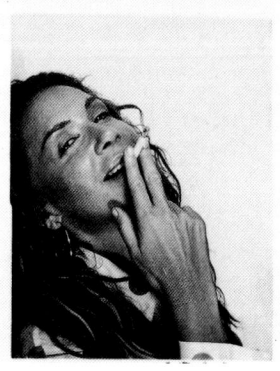

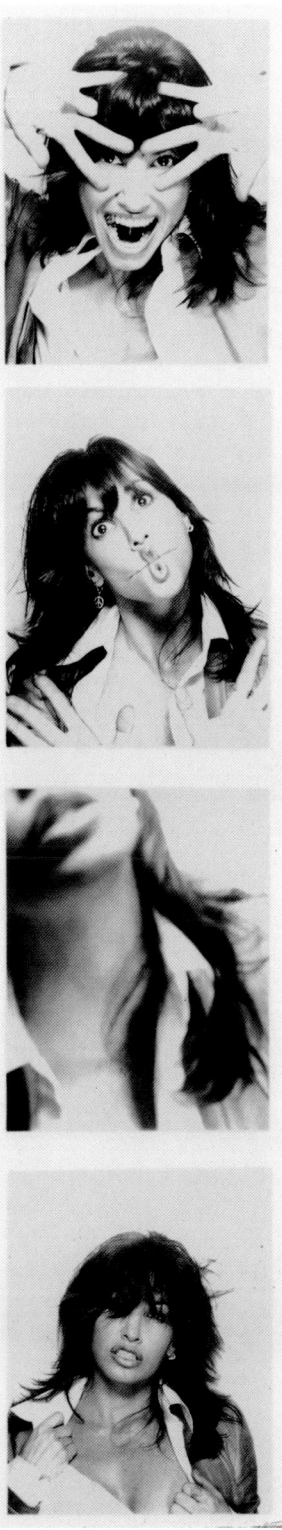

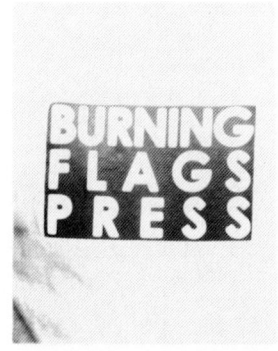
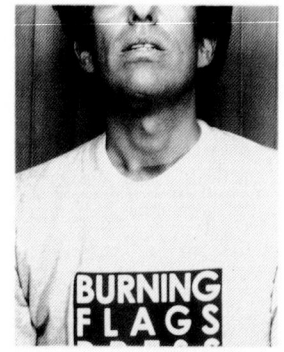
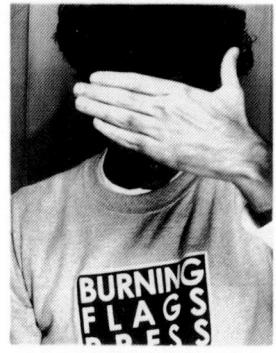
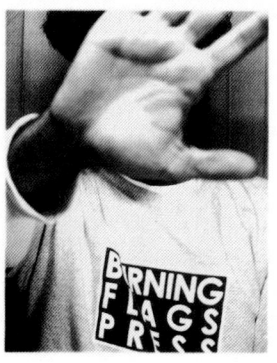

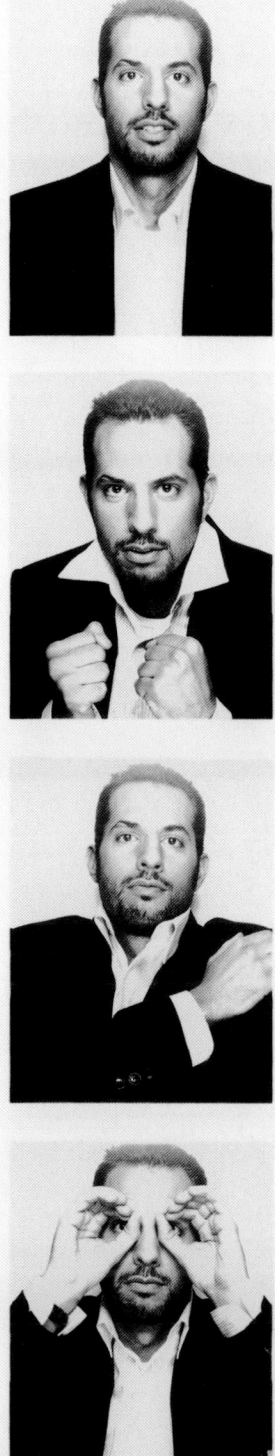

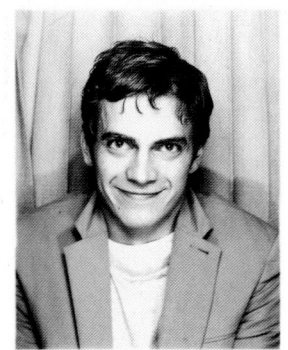

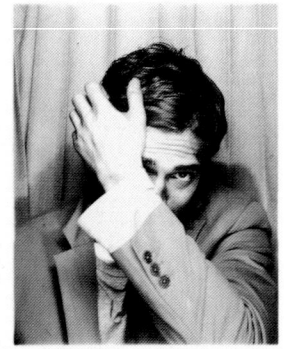

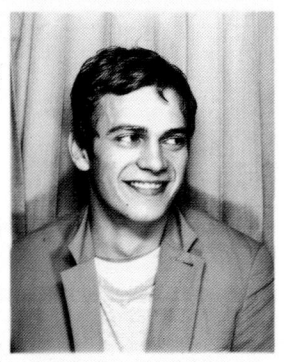

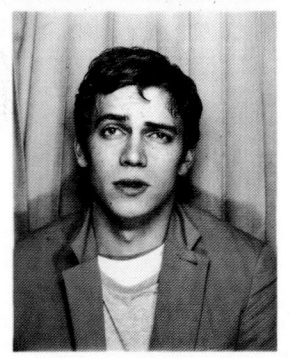

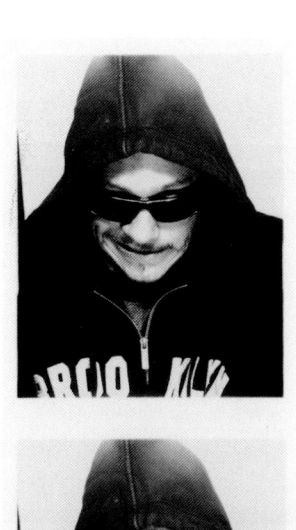
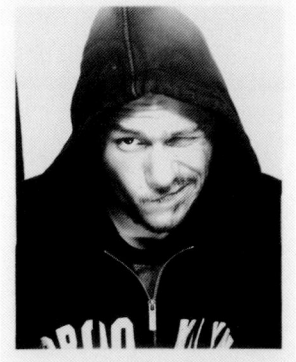
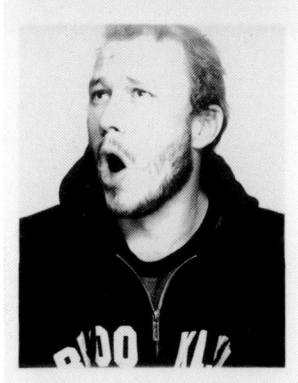
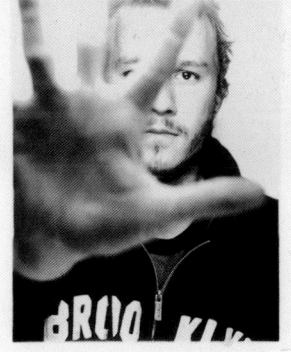

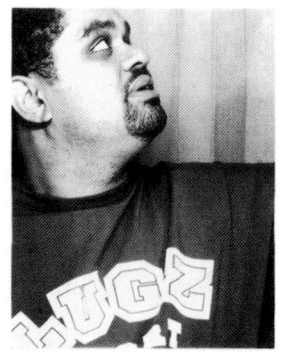

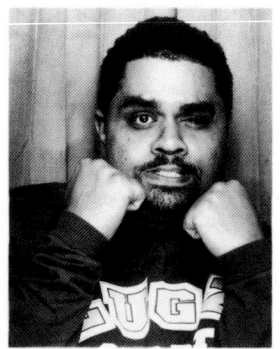

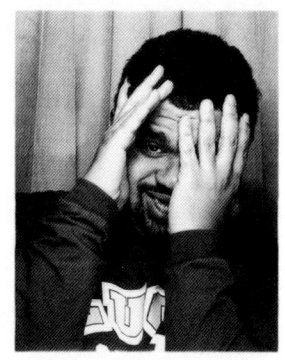

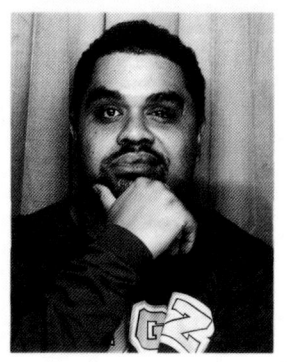

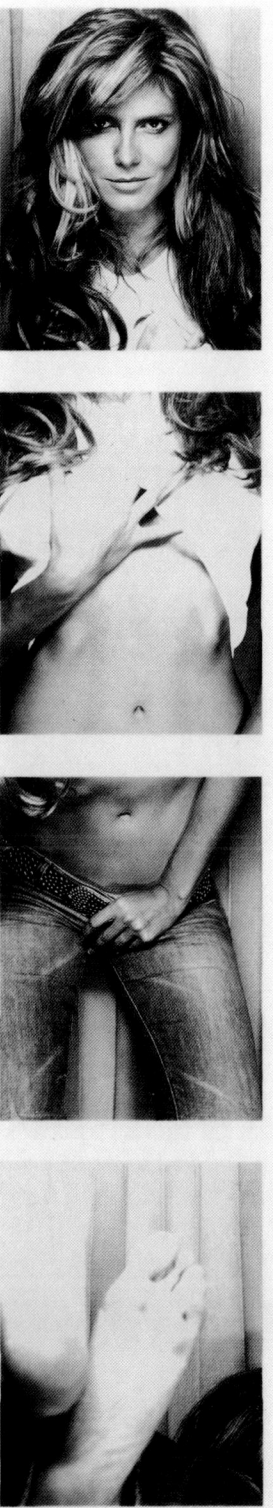

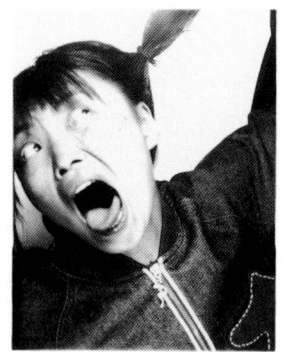

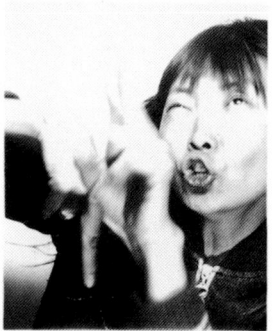

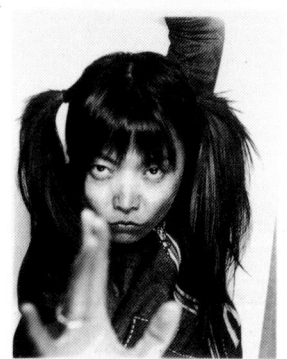

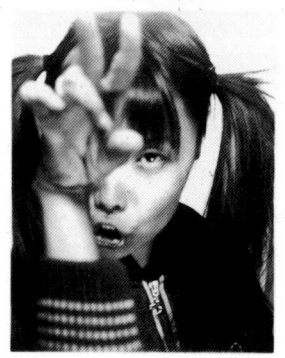

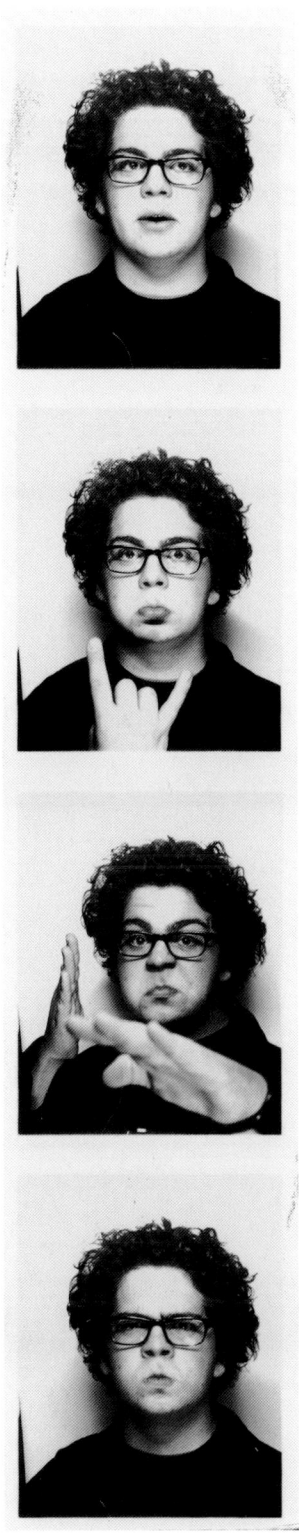

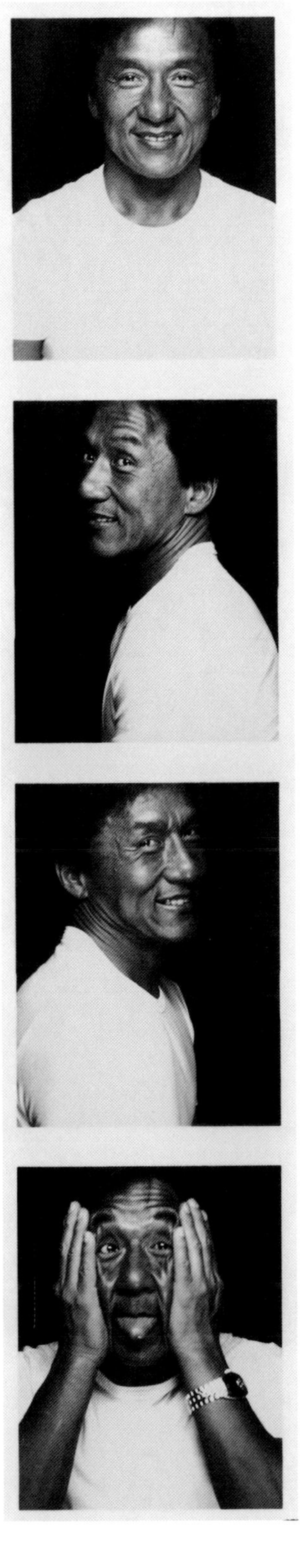

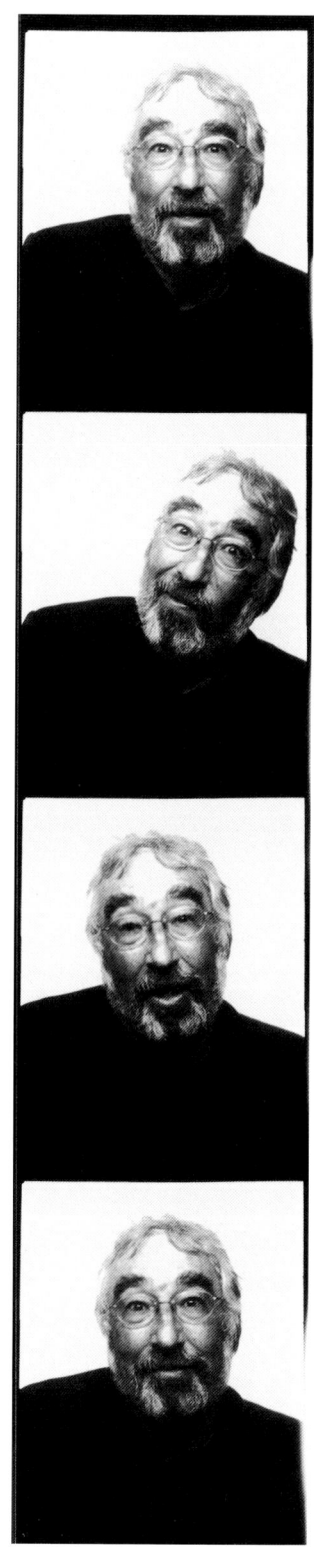

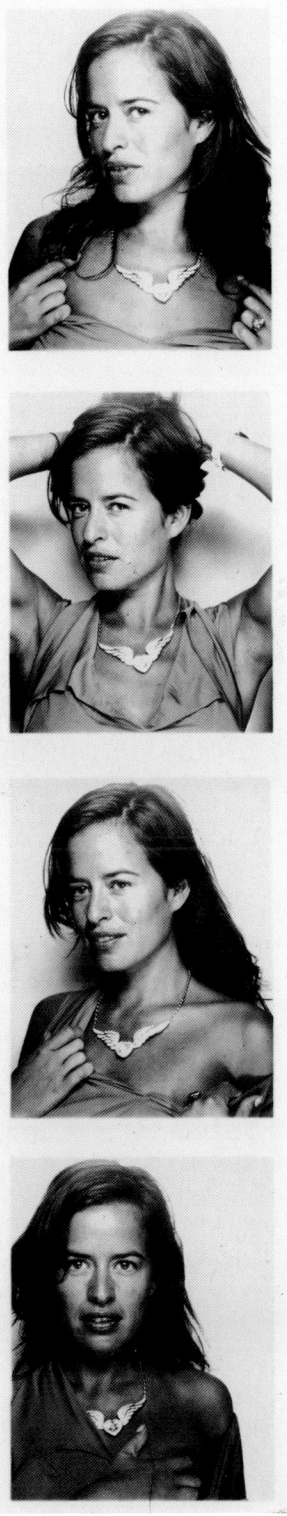

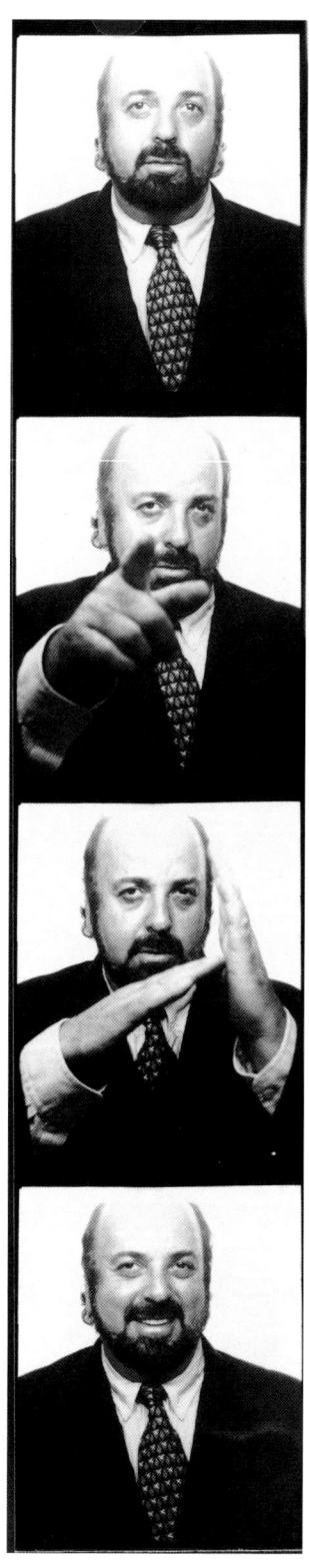

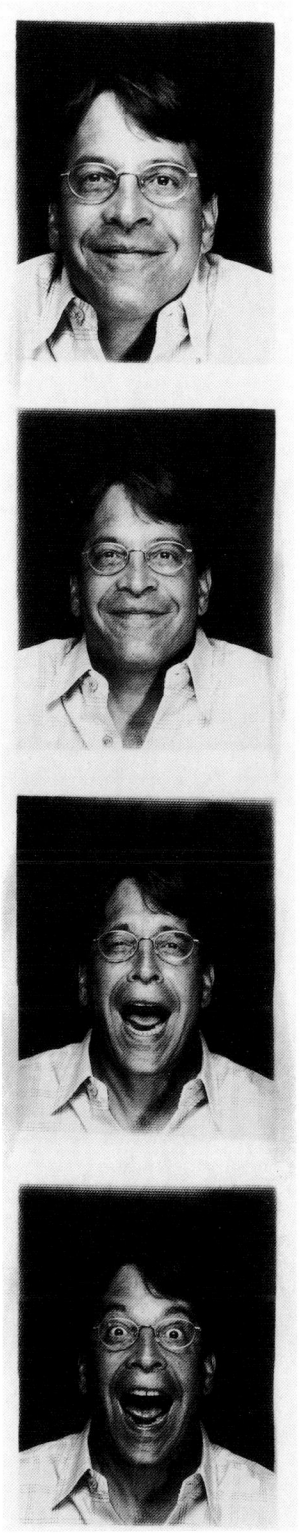

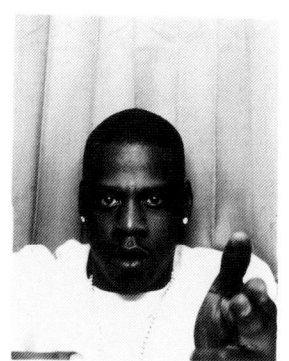

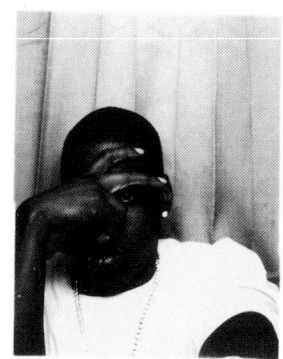

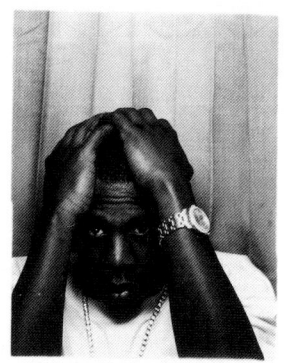

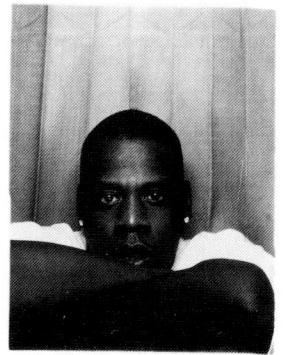

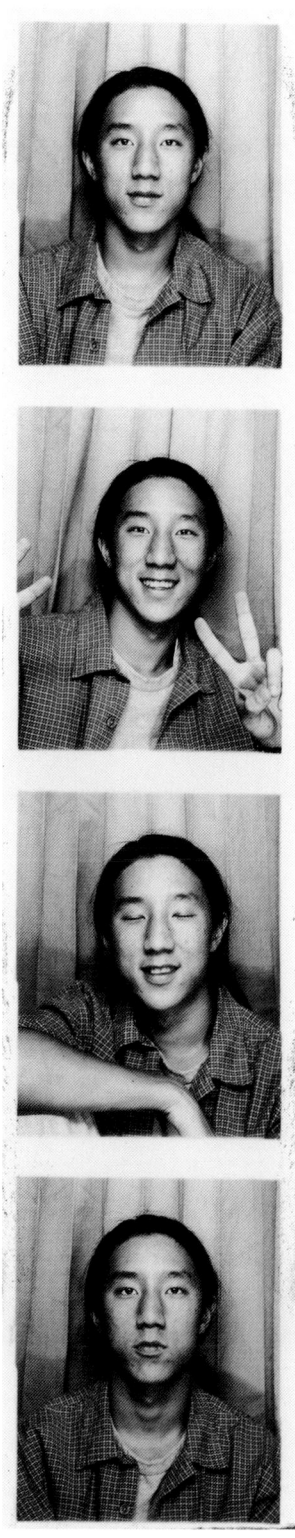

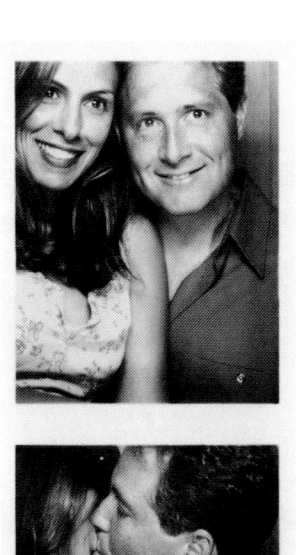
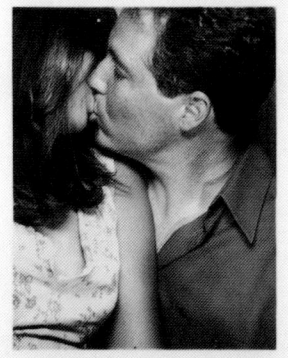
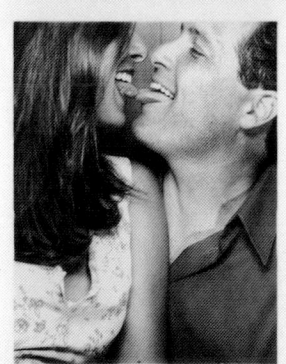
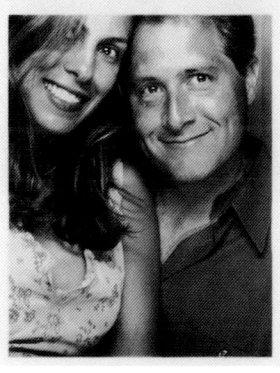

Jeff & Audra Nathanson

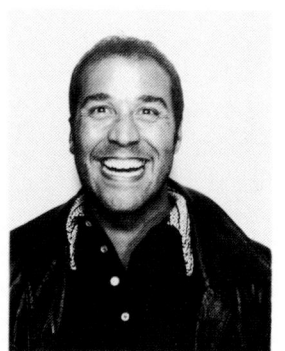

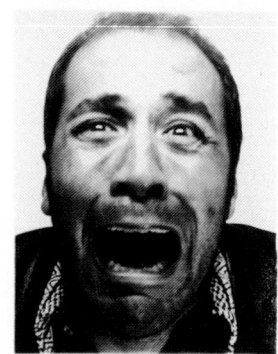

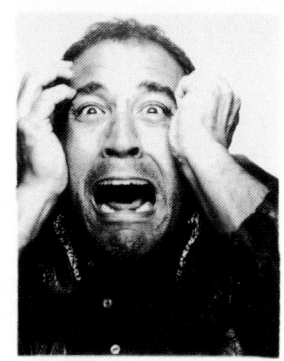

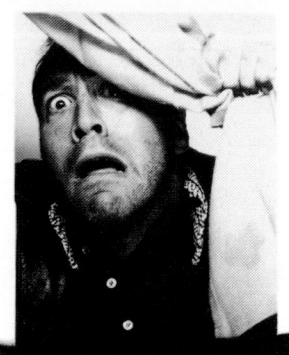

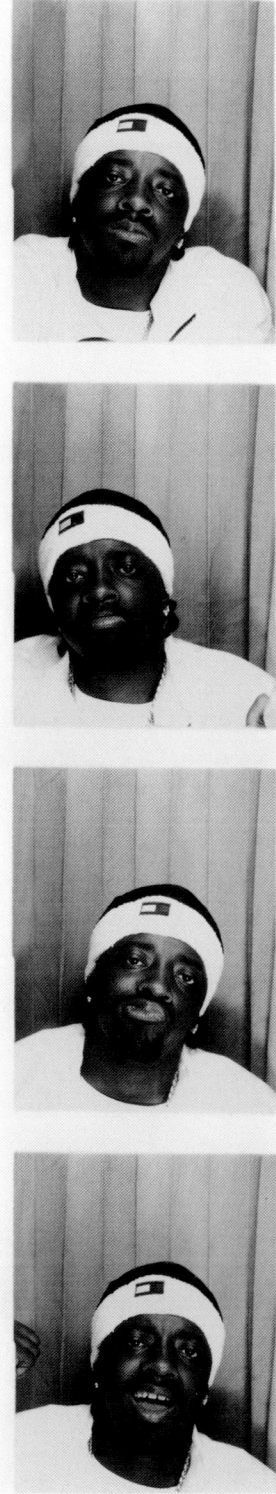

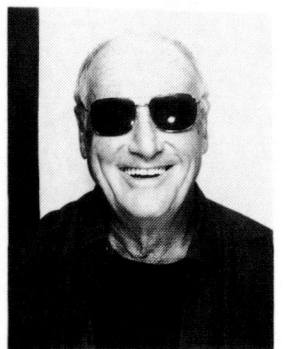

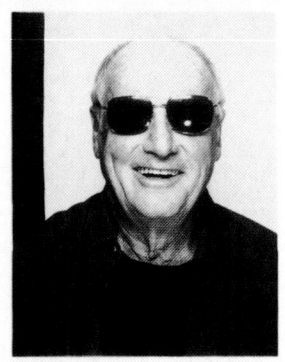

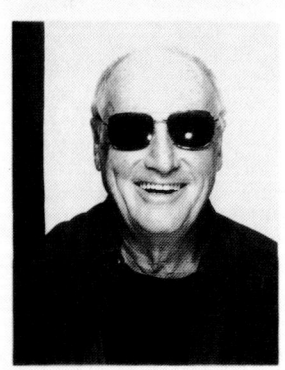

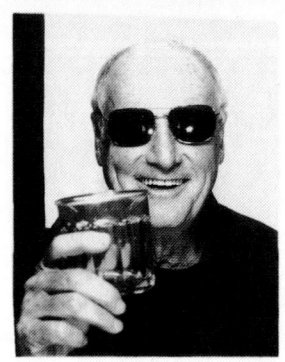

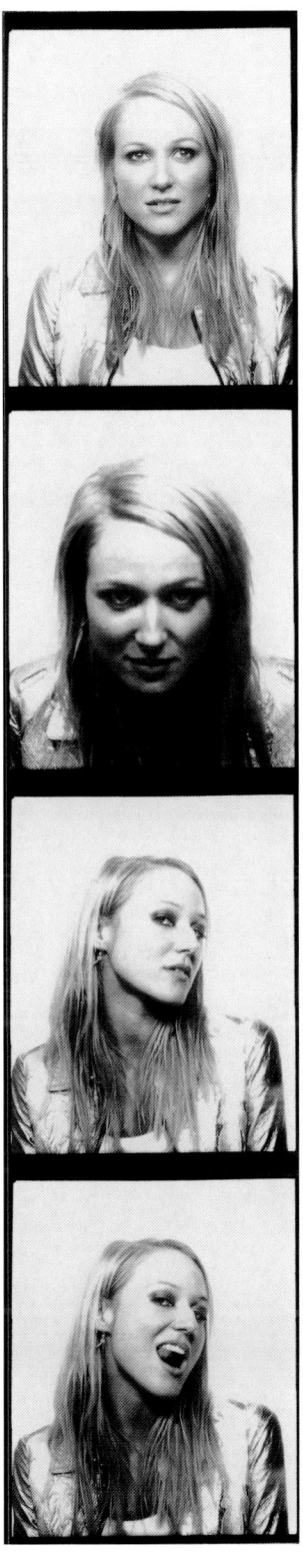

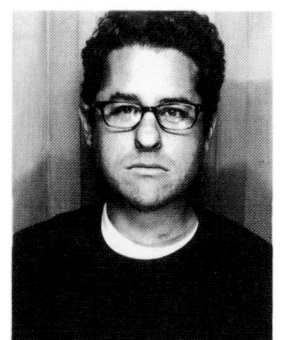
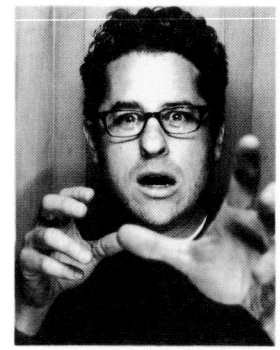
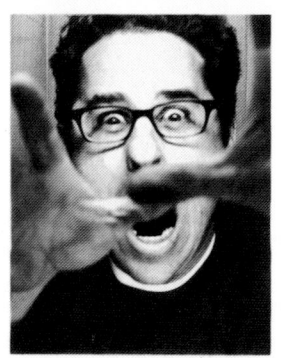
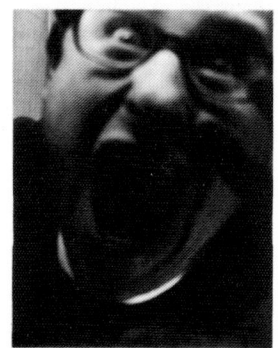

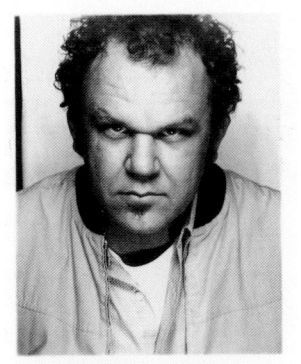
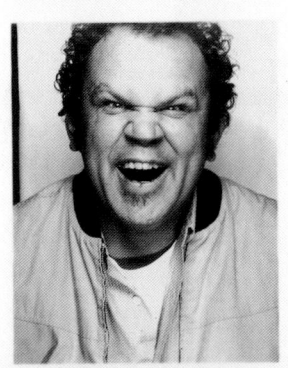
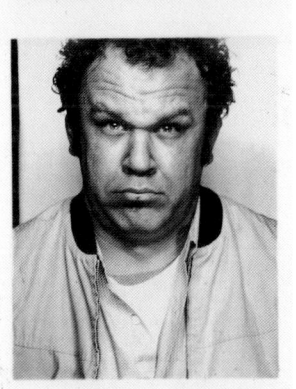
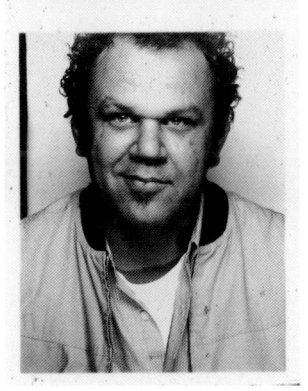

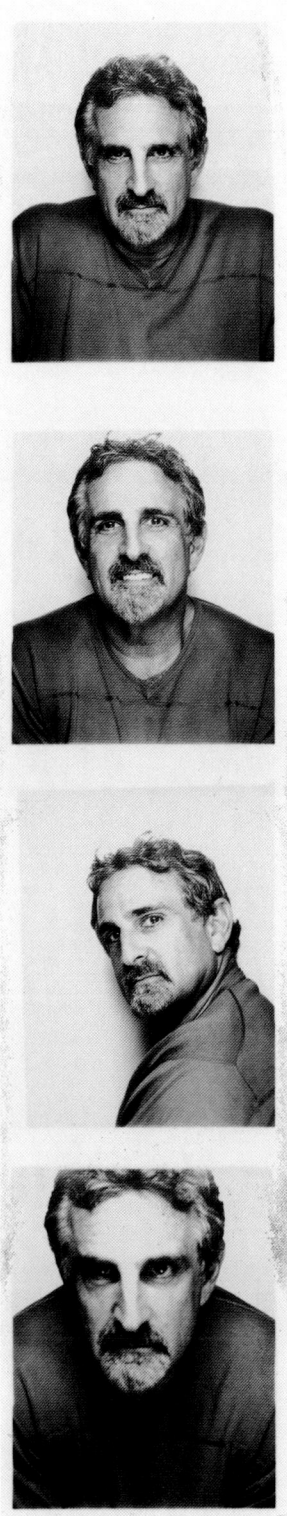

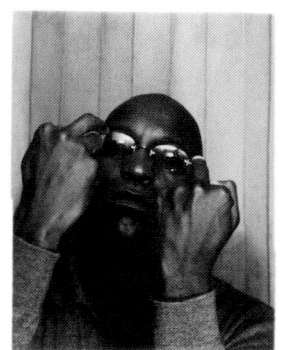

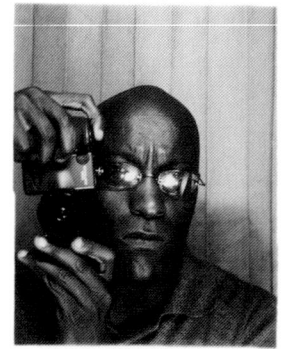

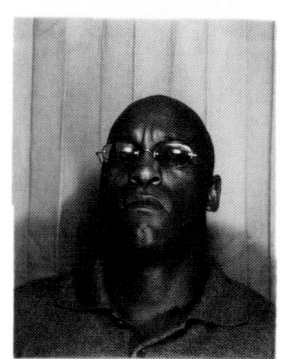

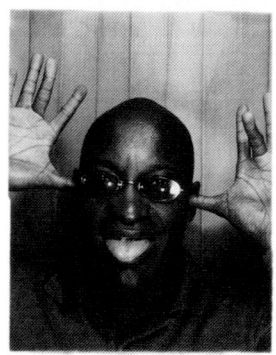

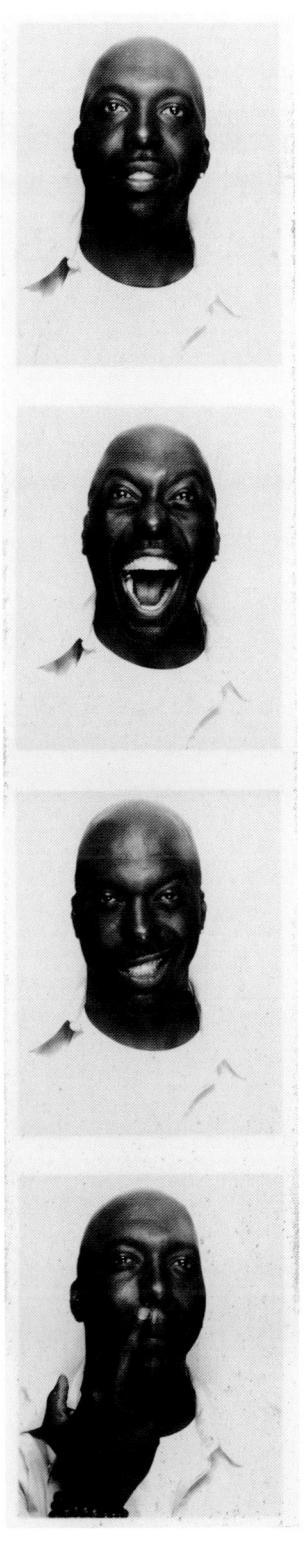

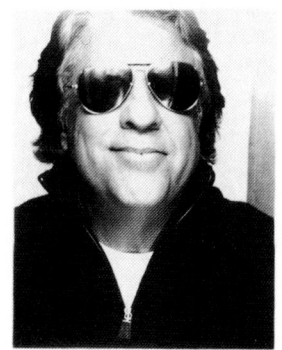
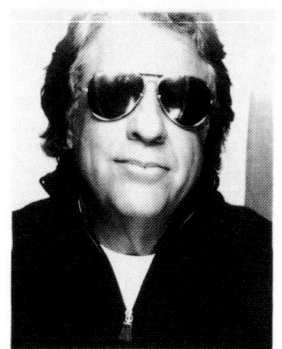
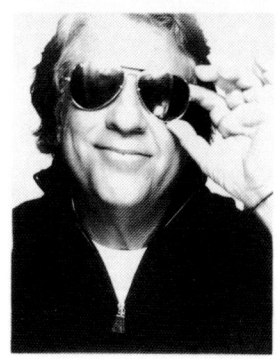
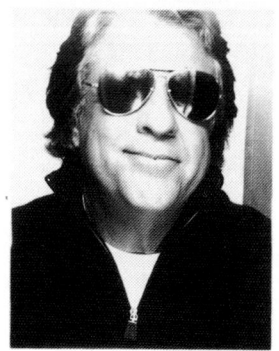

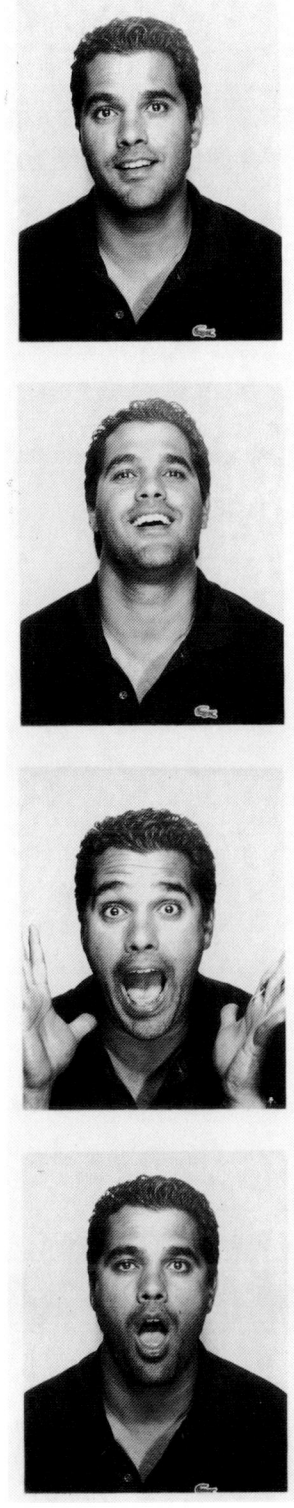

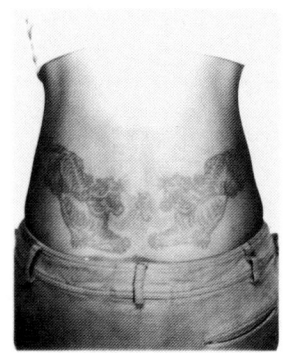

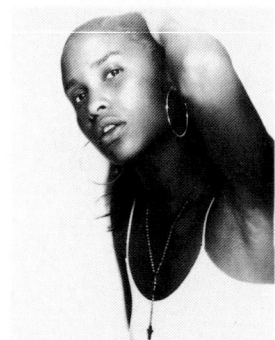

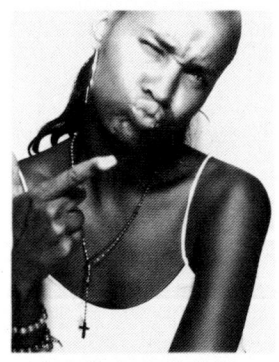

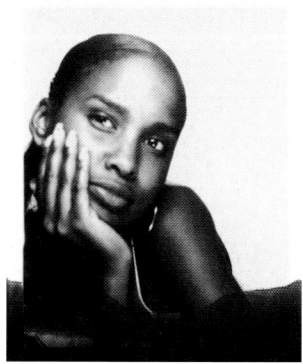

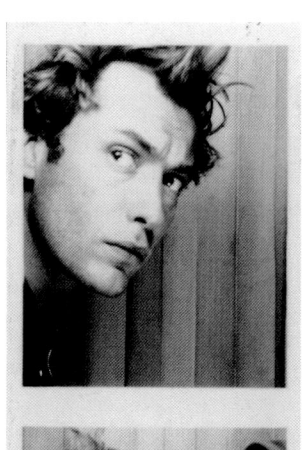
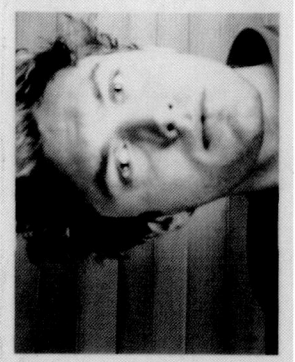
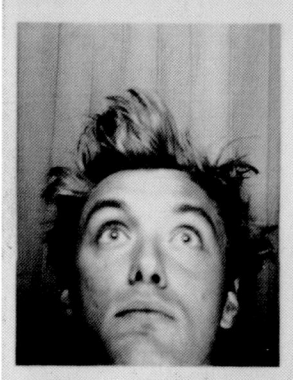
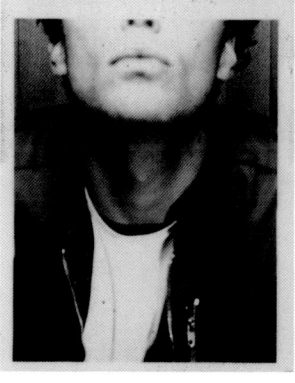

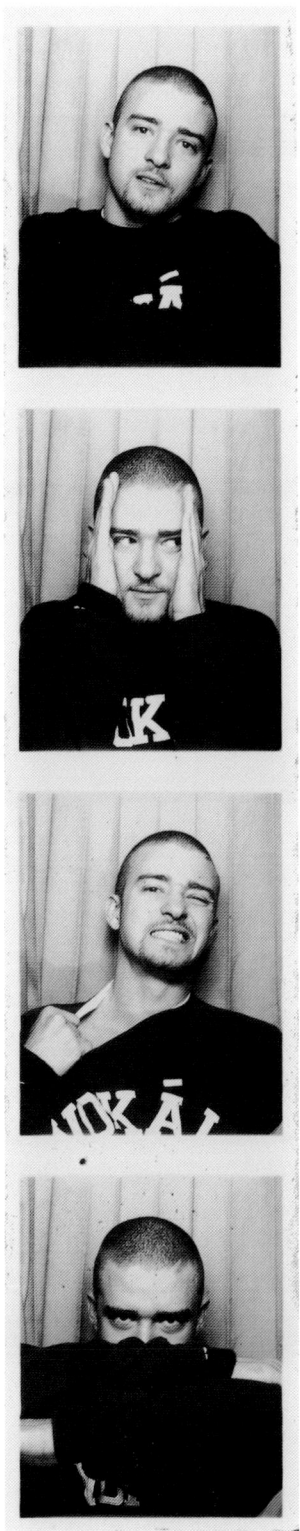

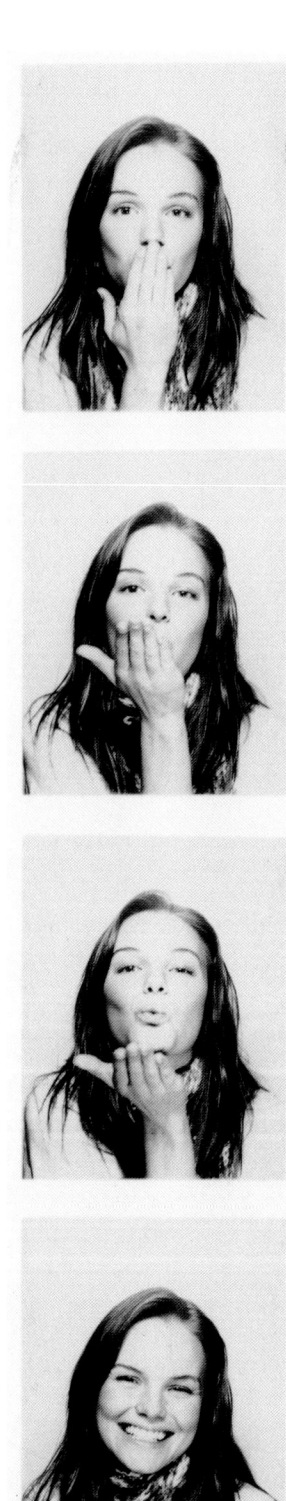

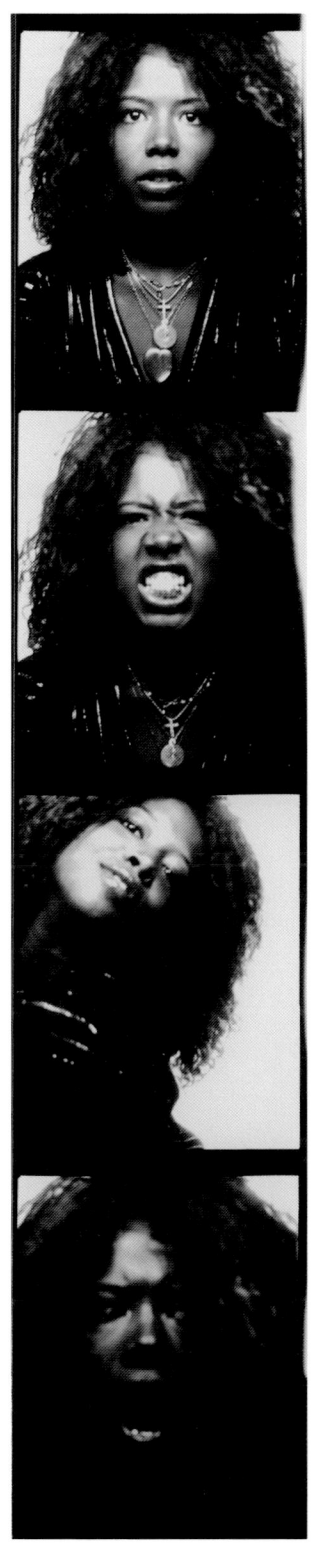

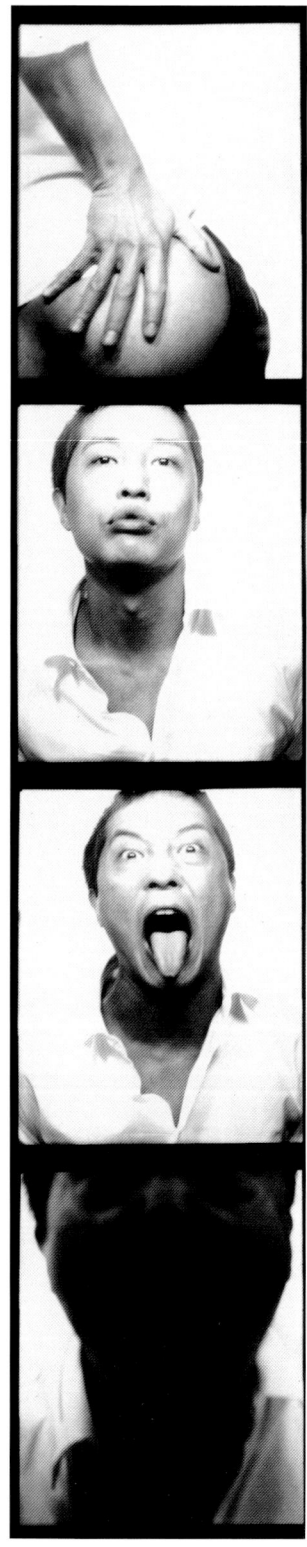

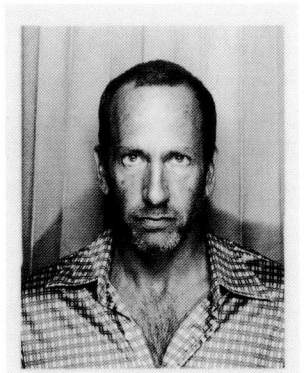
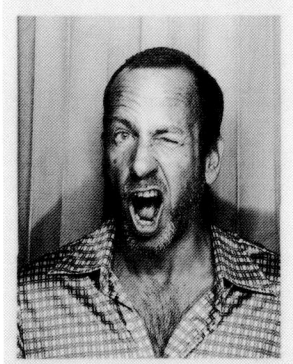
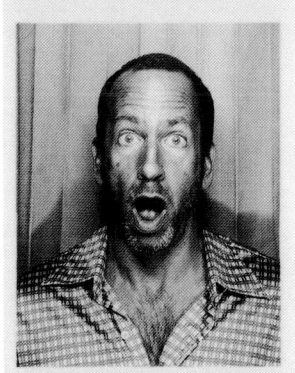
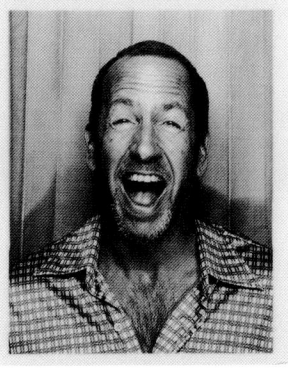

Kenny Scharf

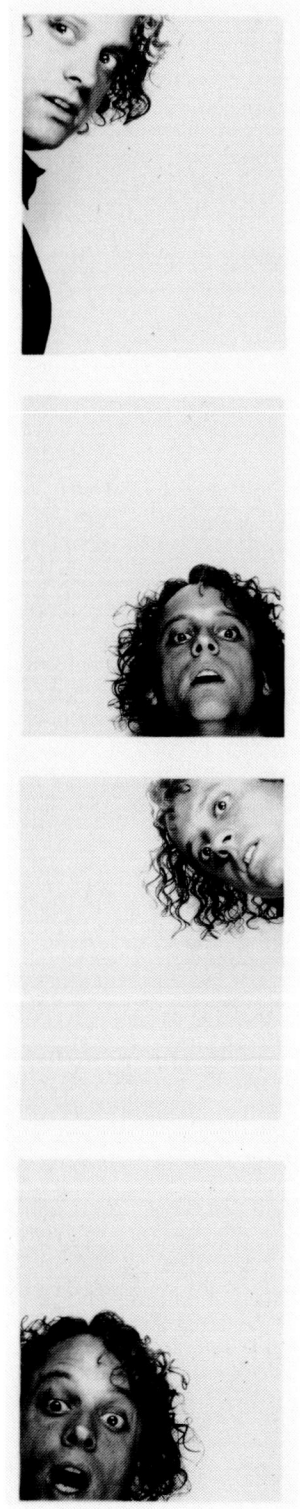

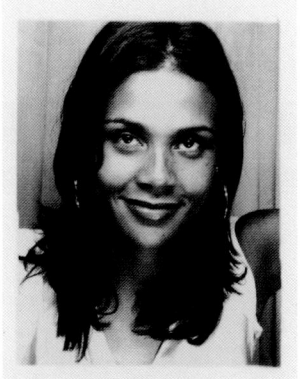
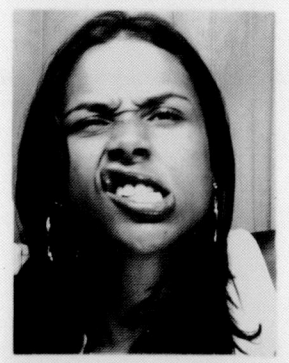
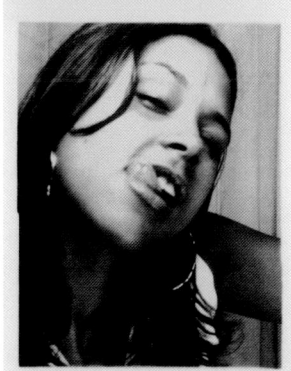
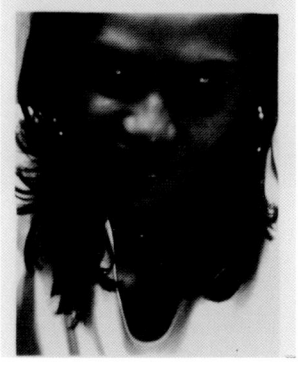

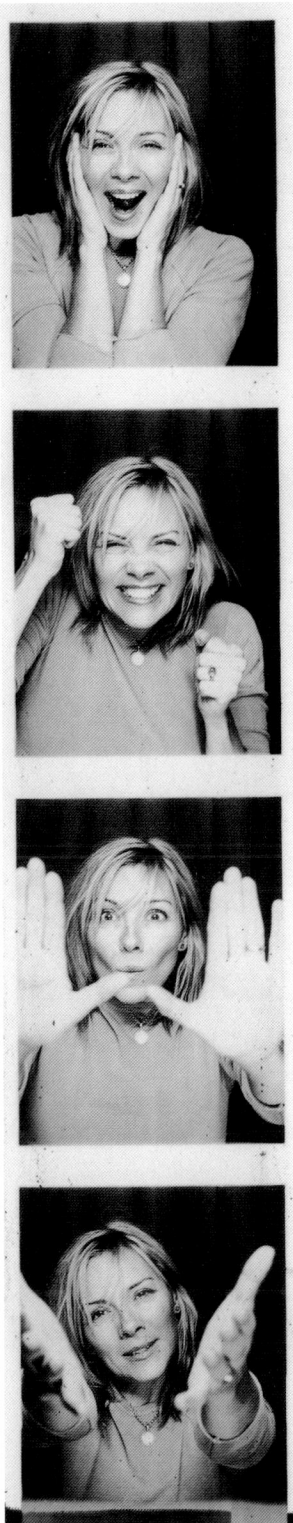

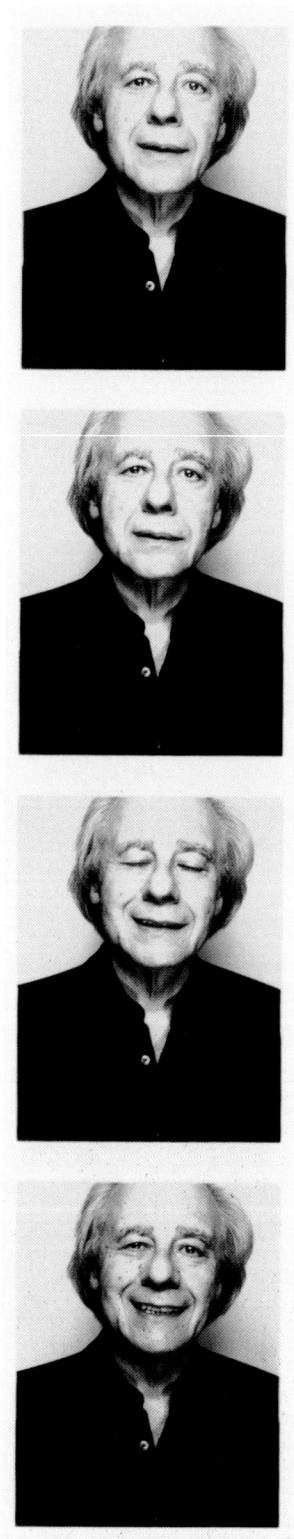

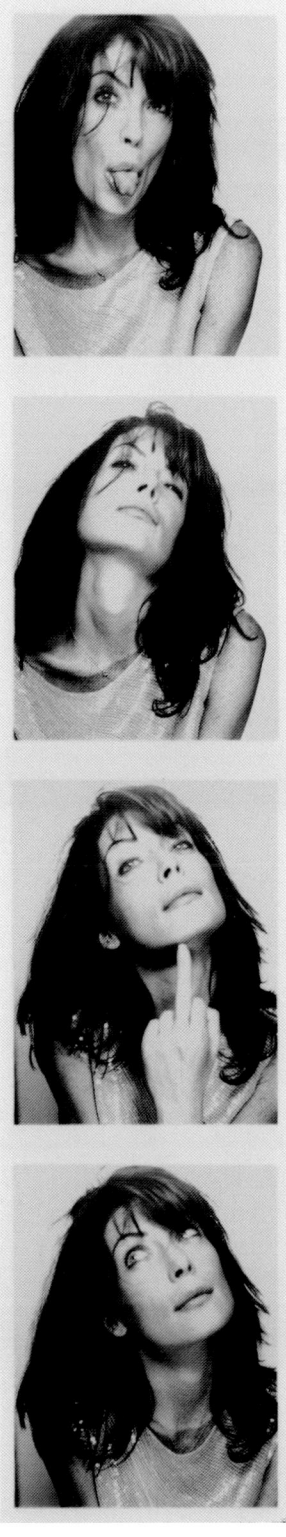

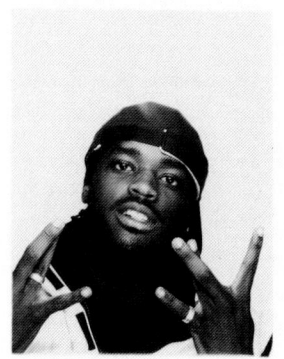
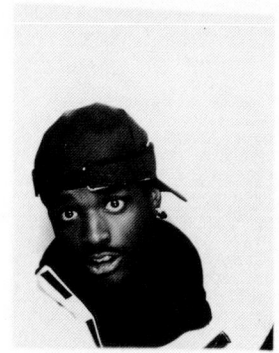
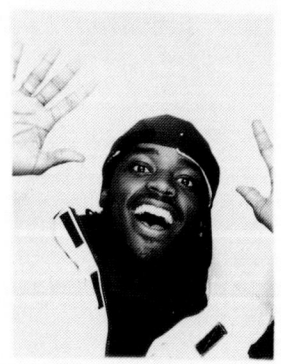
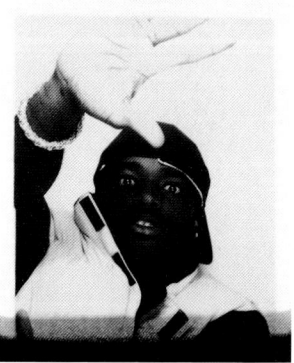

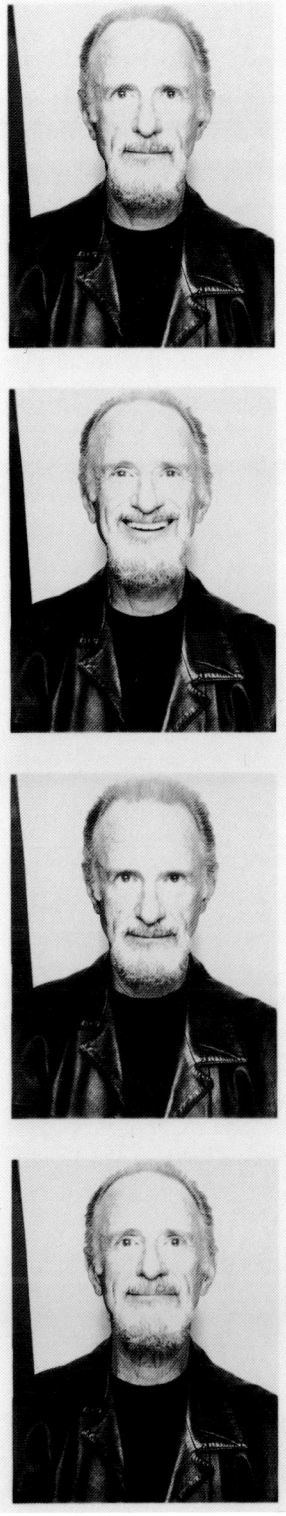

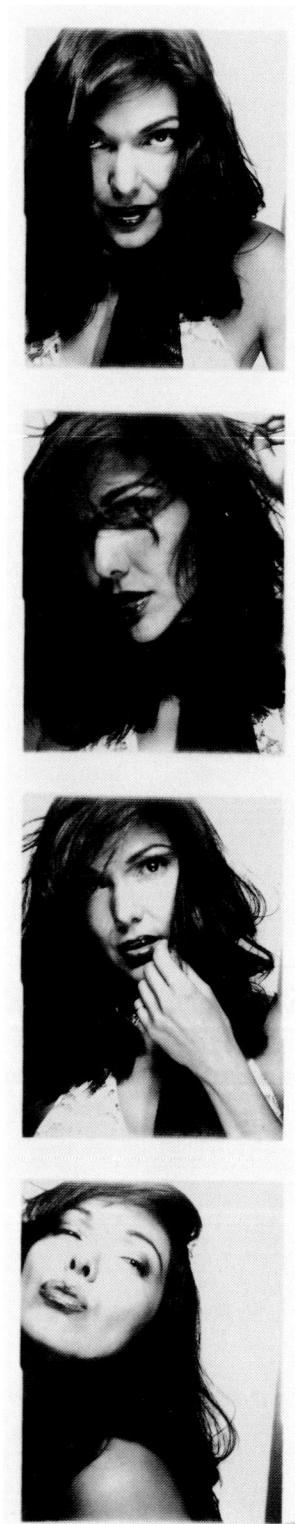

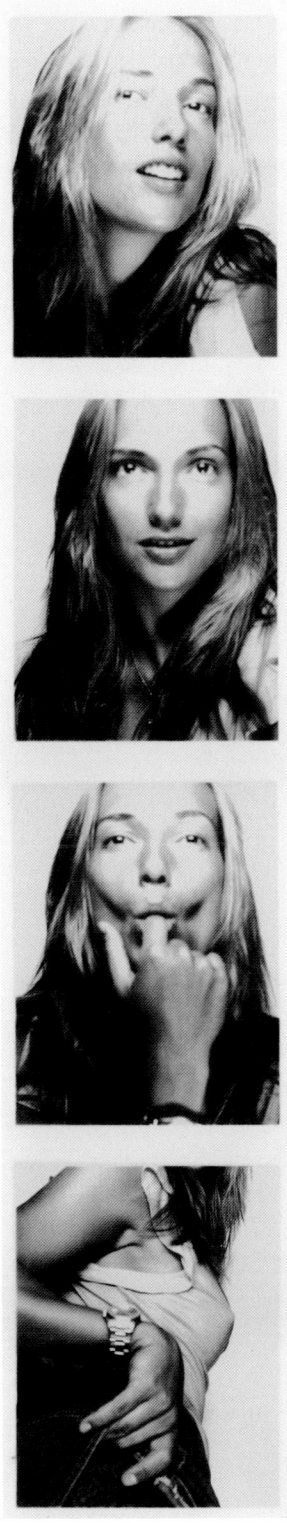

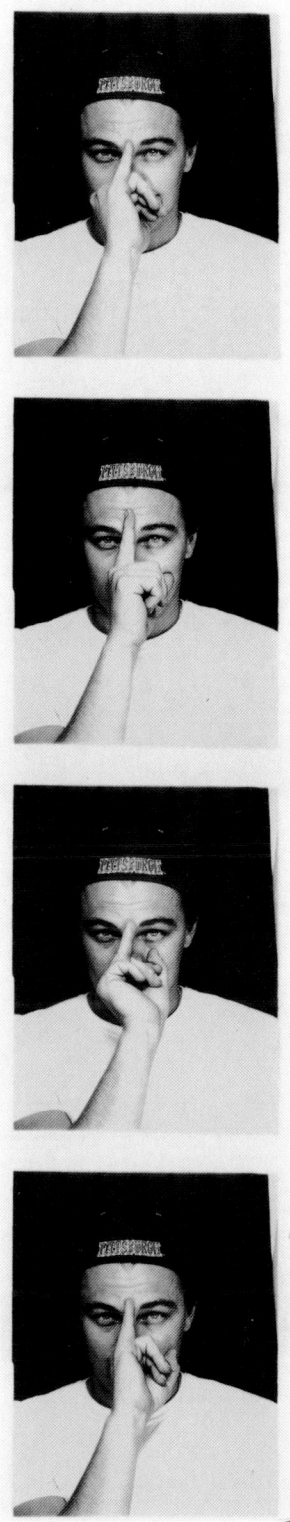

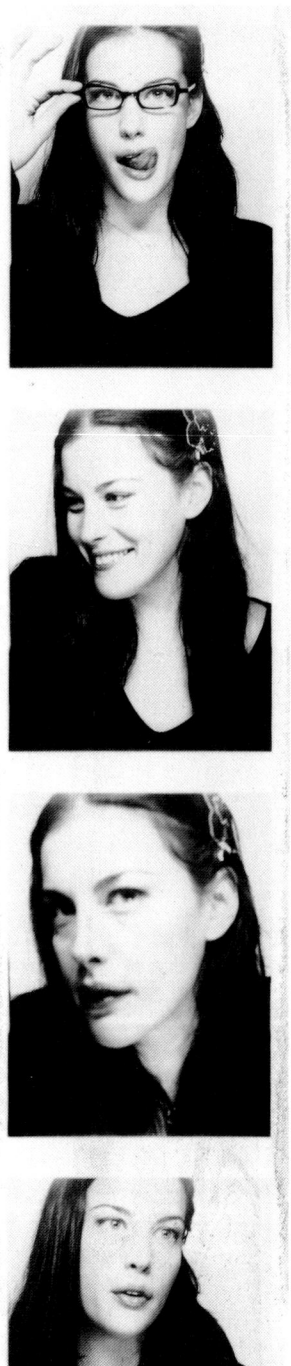

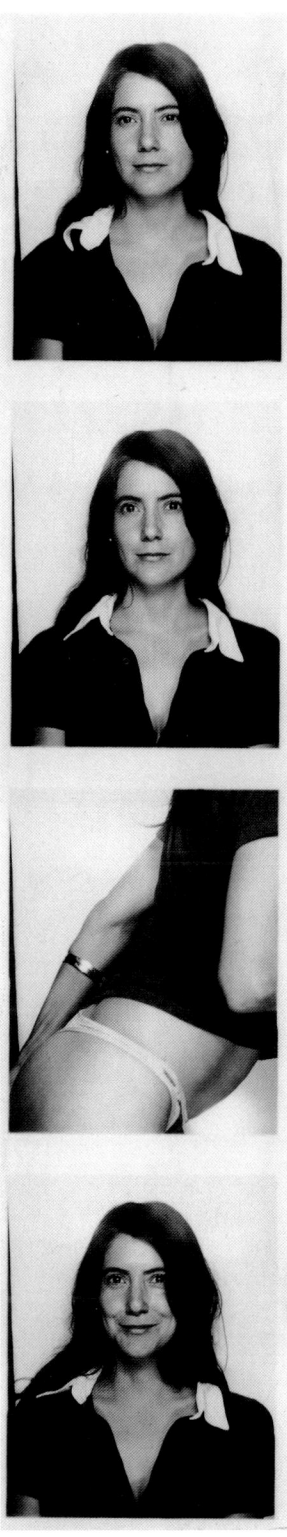

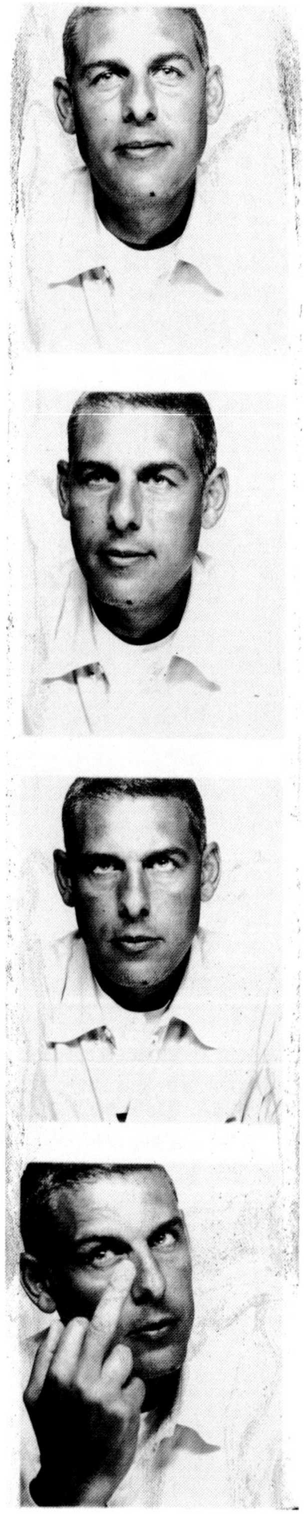

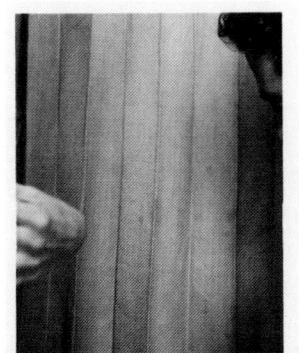
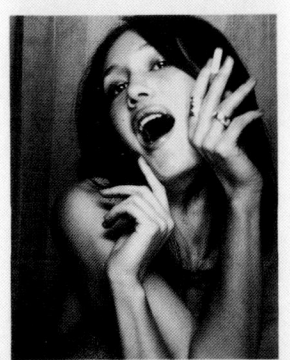
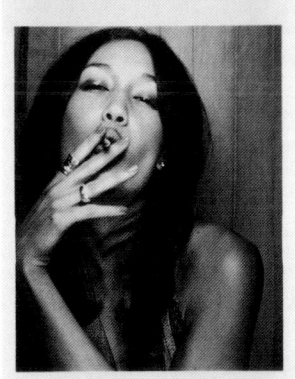
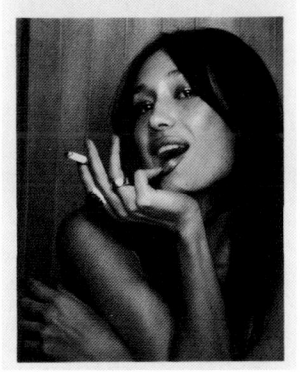

Maggie Q

127

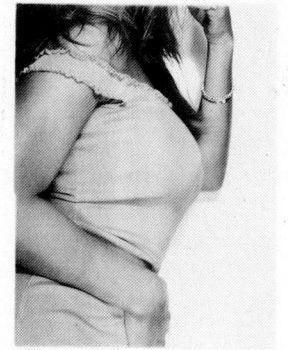
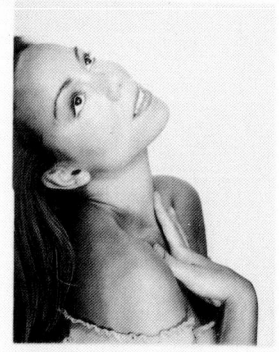
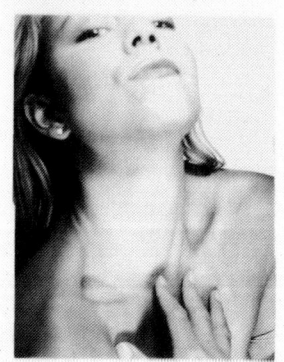
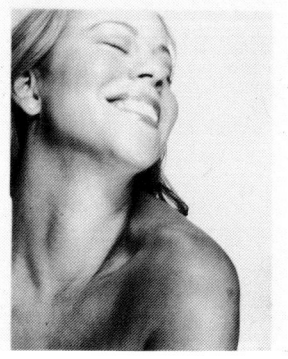

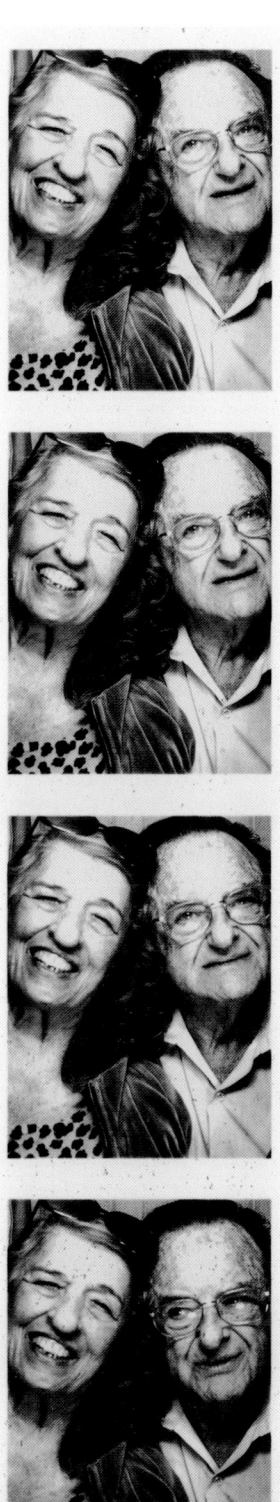

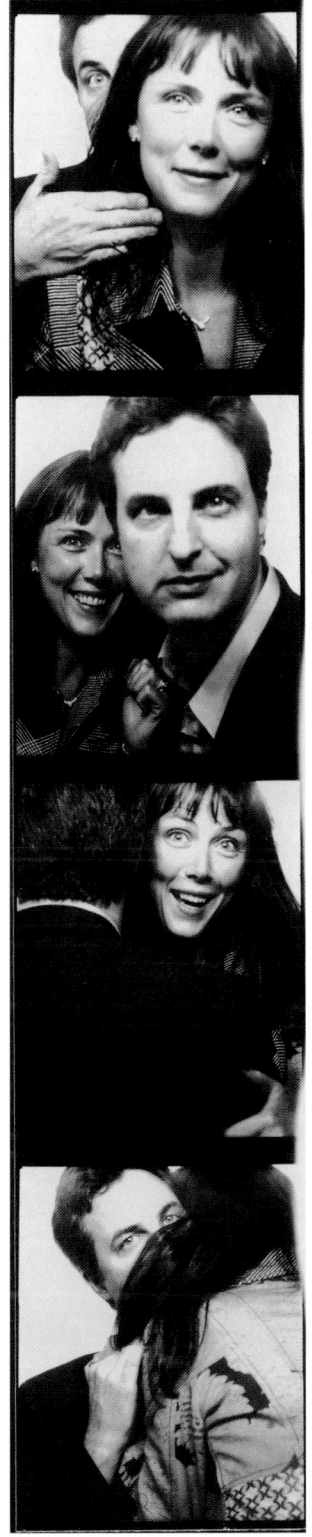

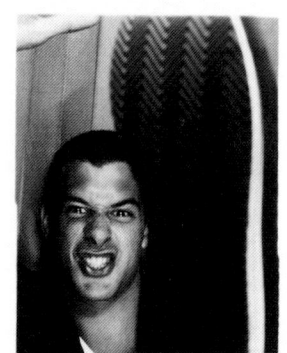
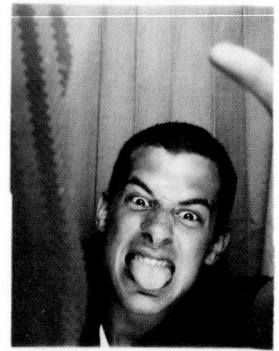
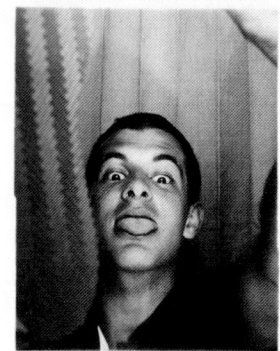
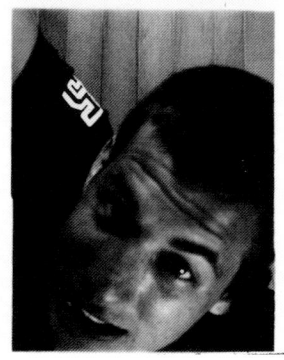

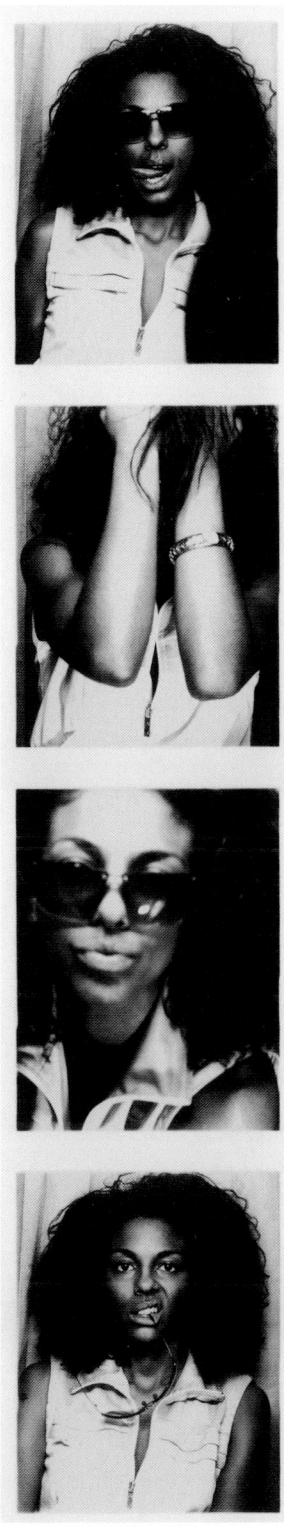

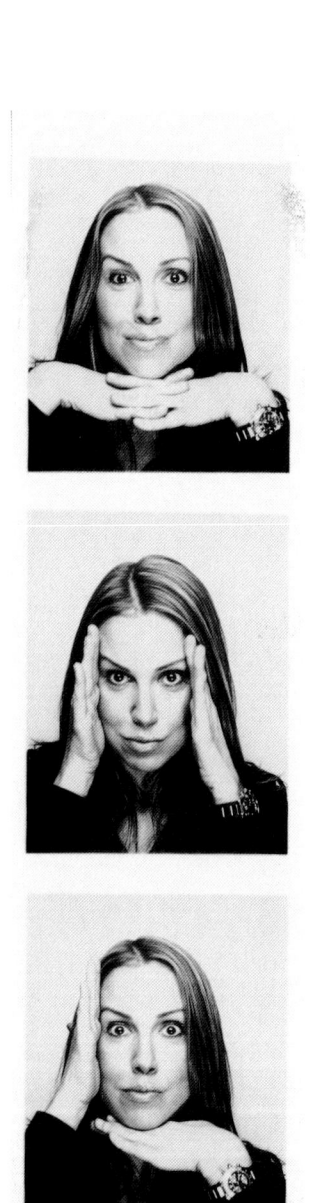

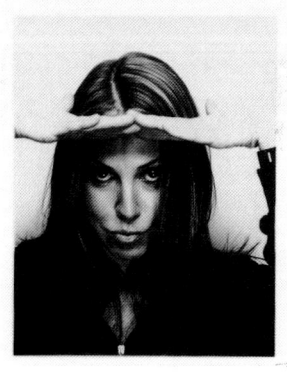

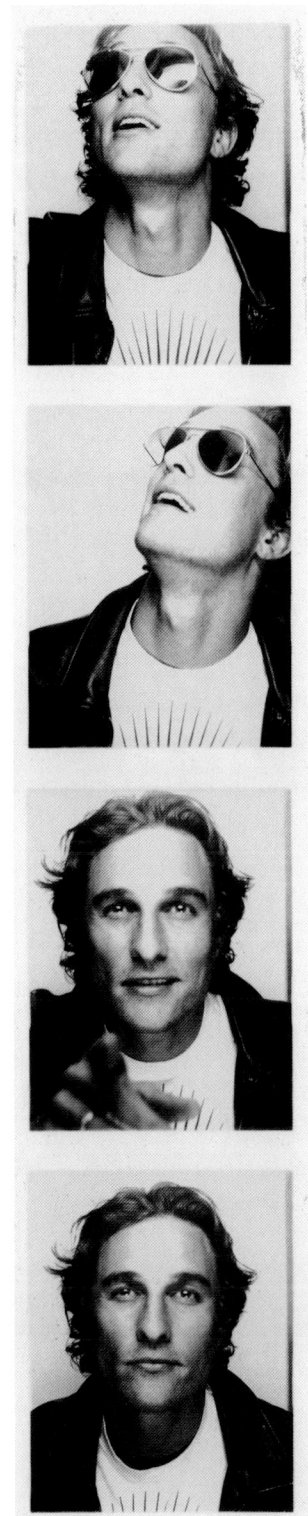

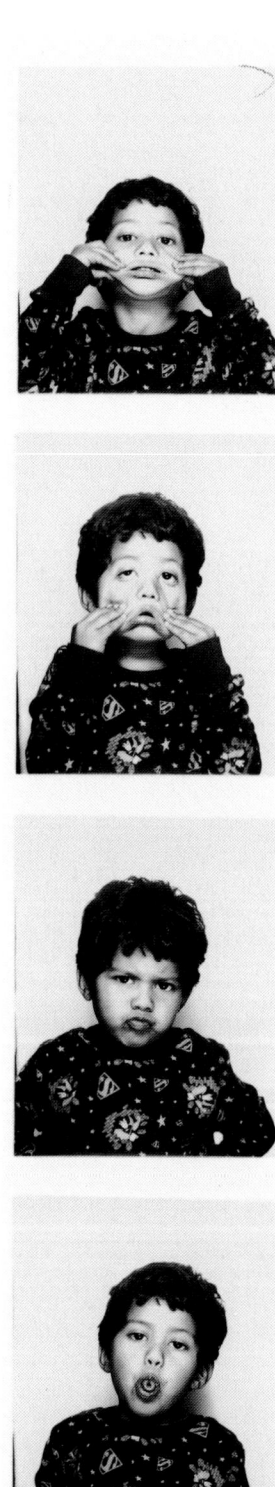

Max Pratts

136

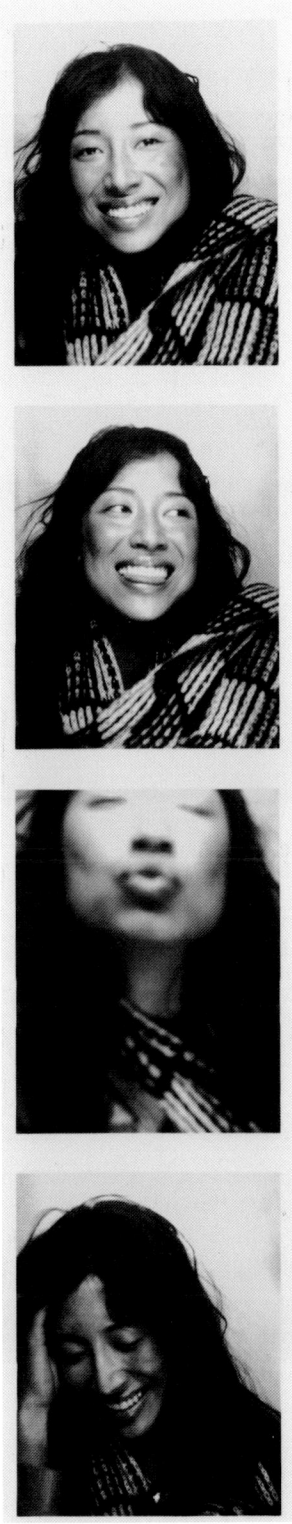

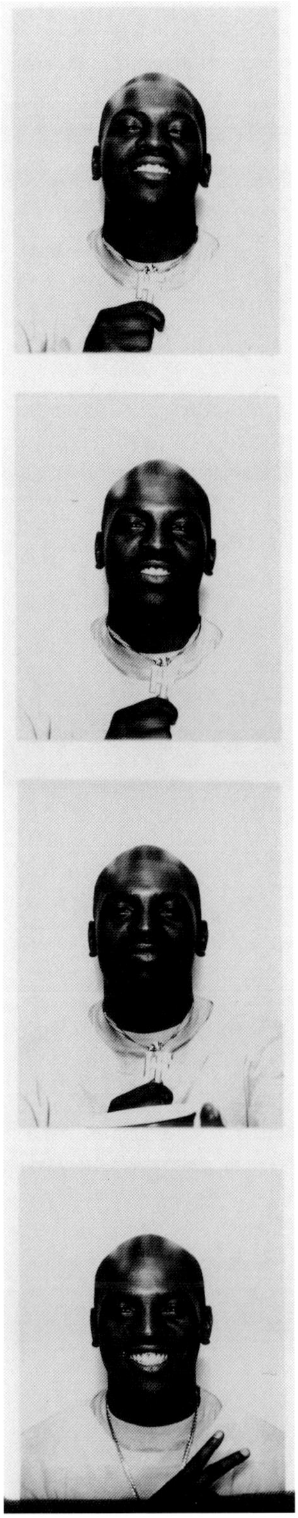

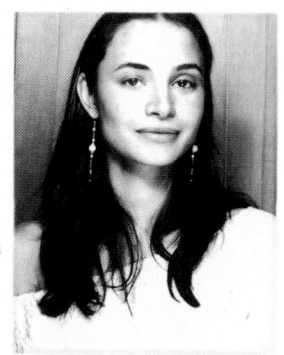

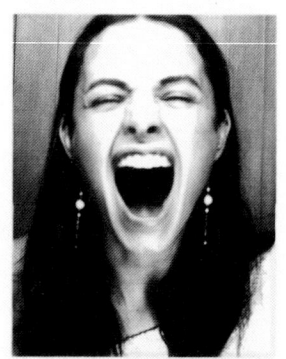

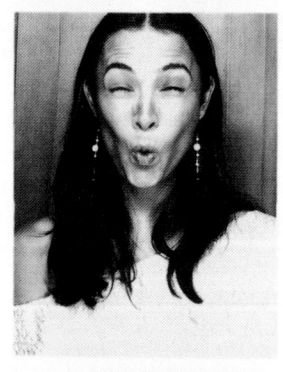

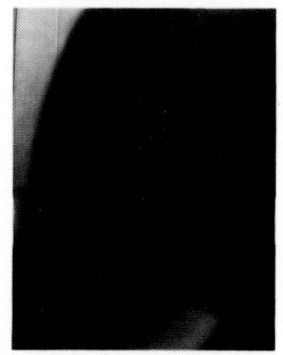

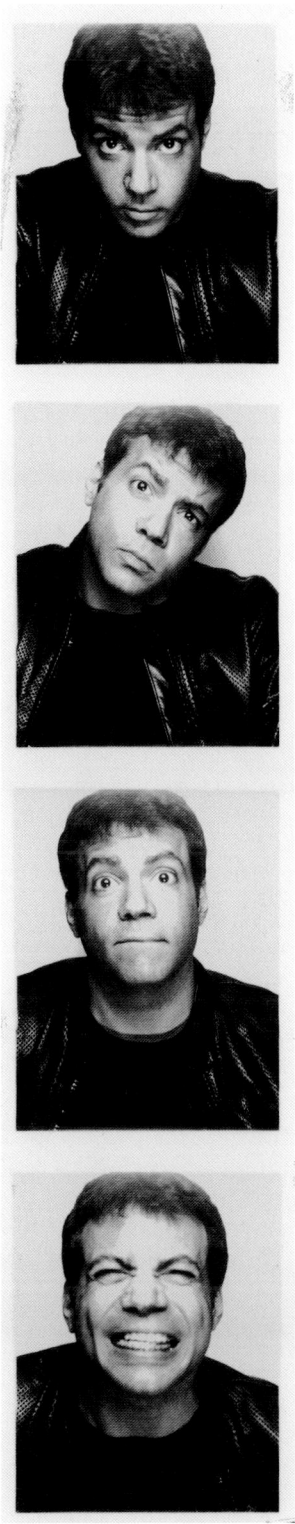

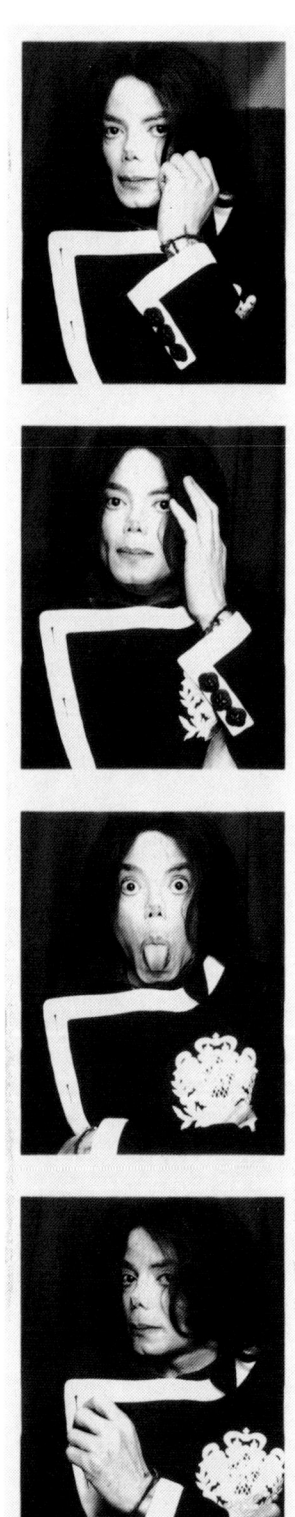

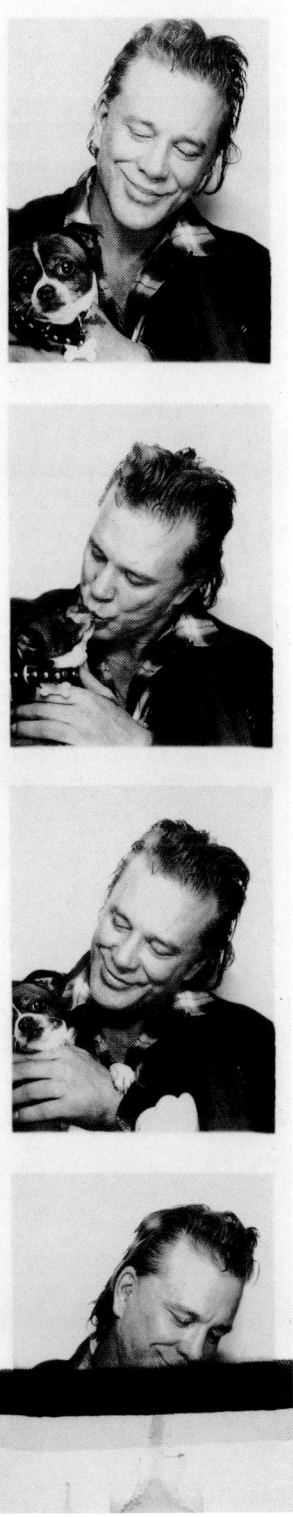

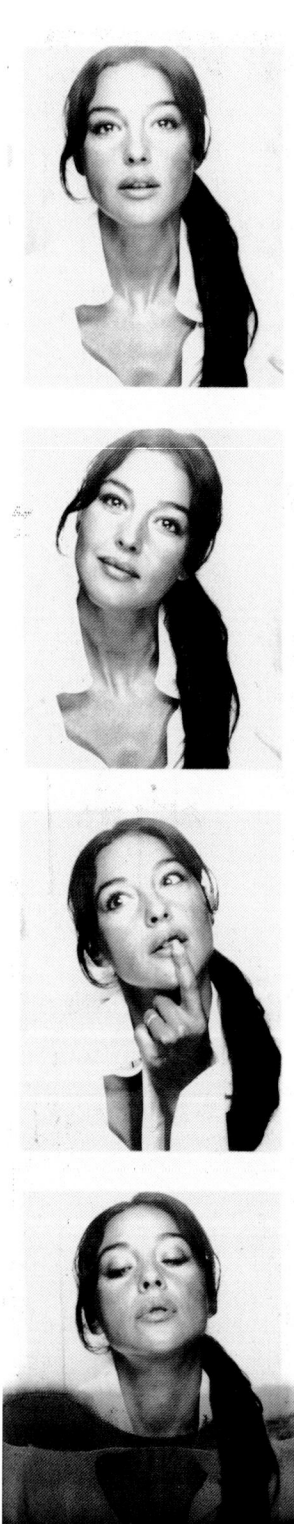

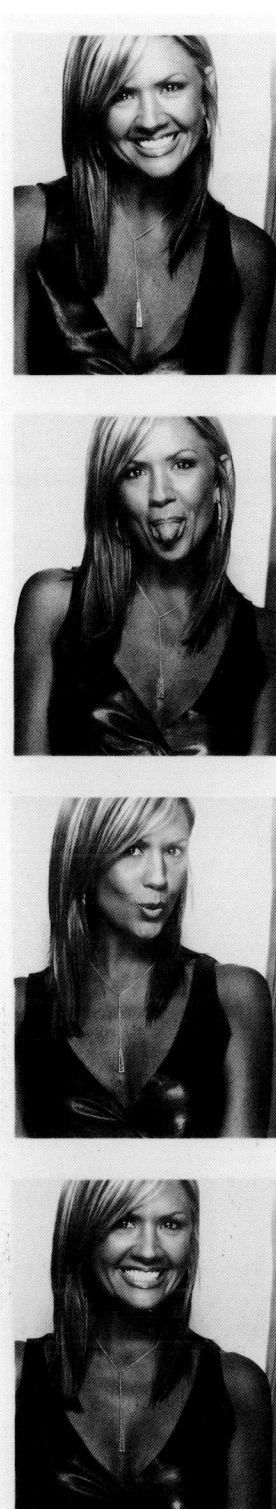

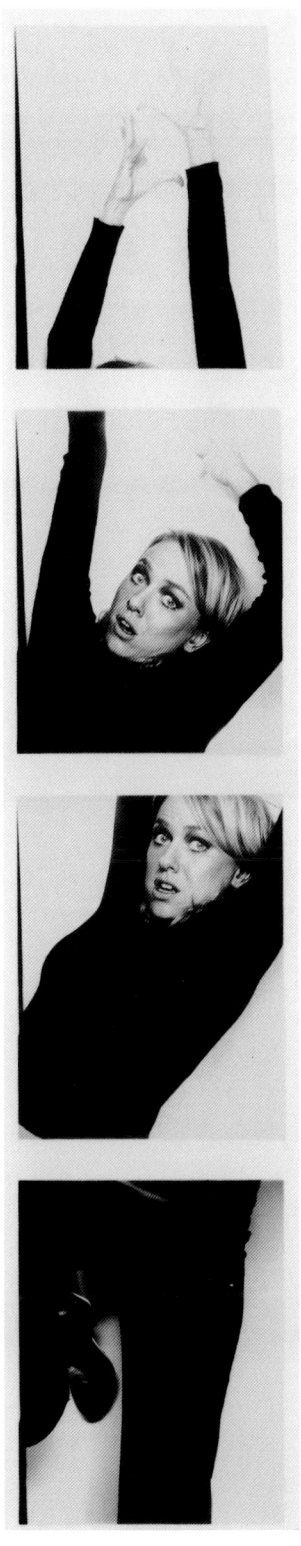

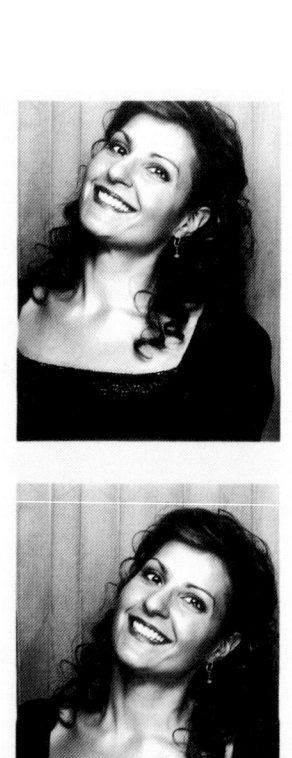
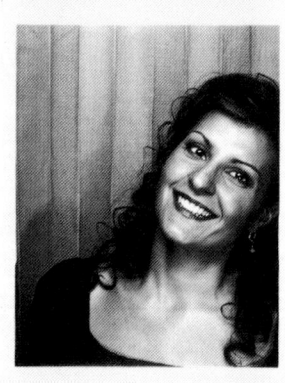
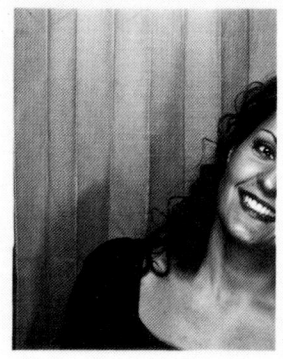

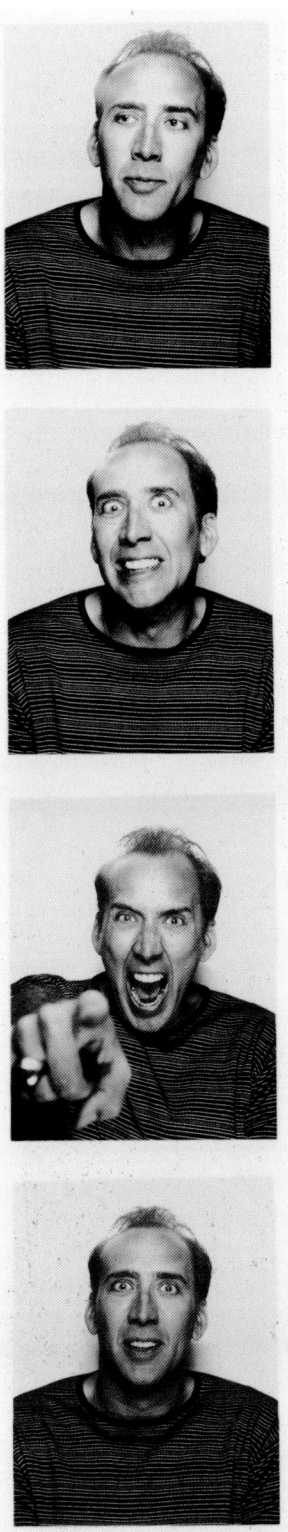

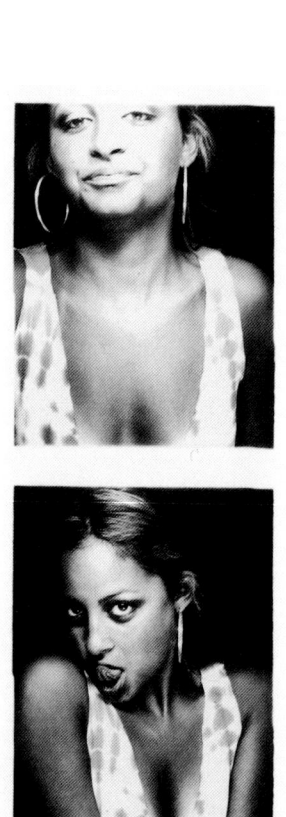
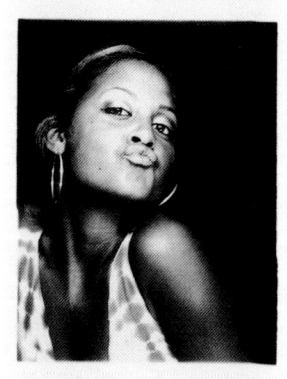
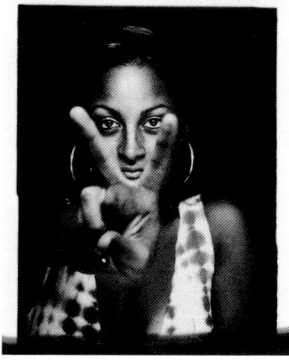

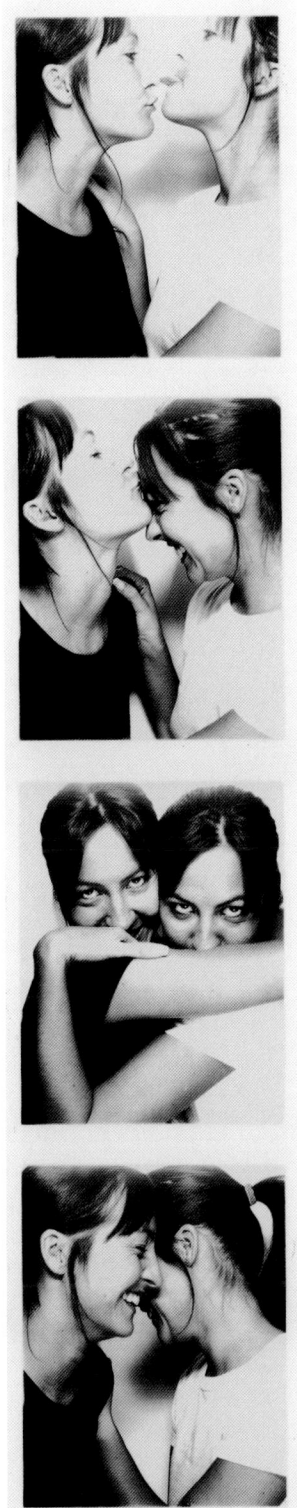

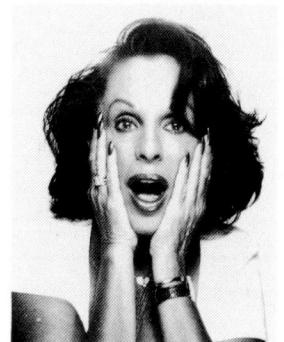

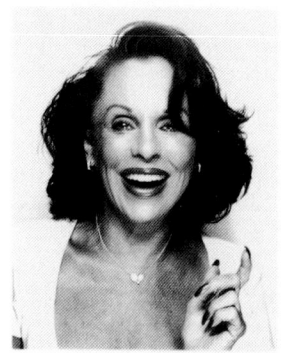

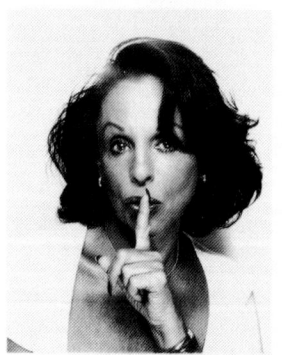

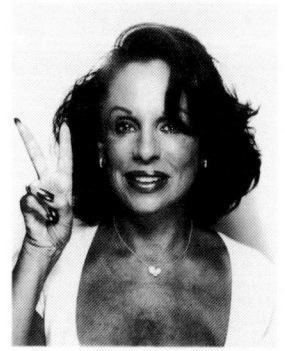

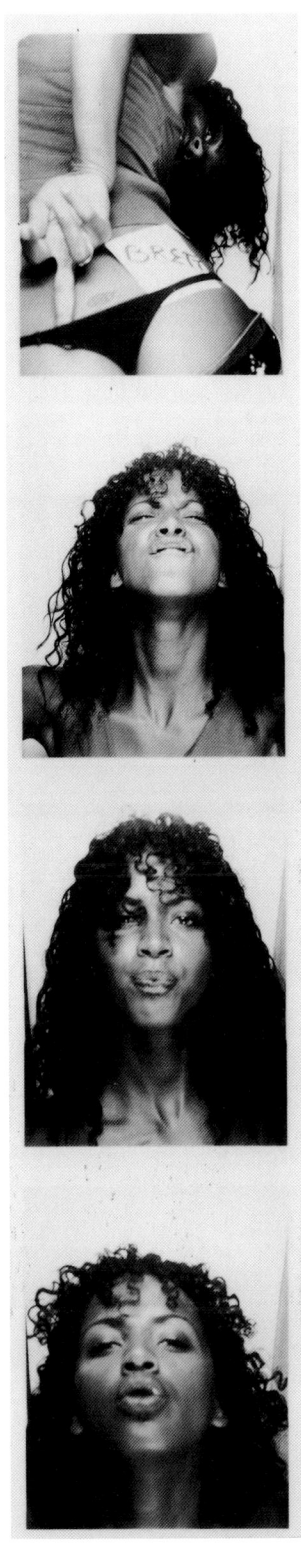

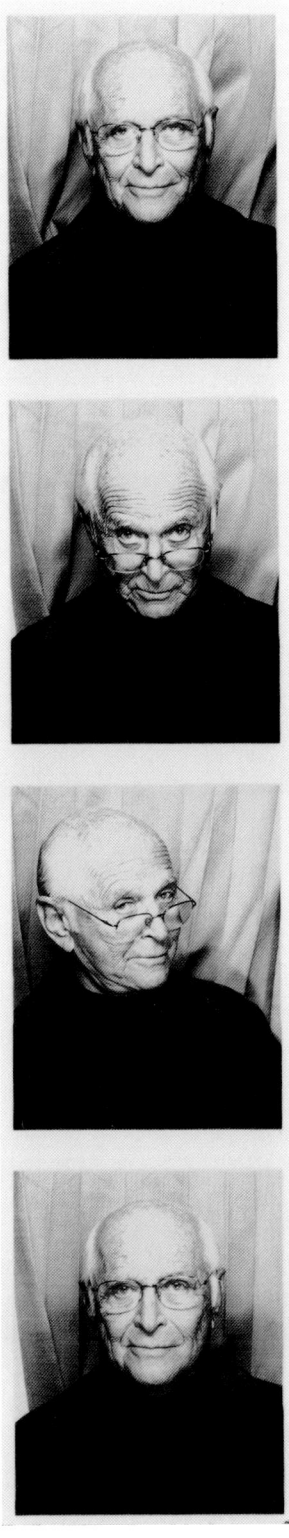

Norman Lear

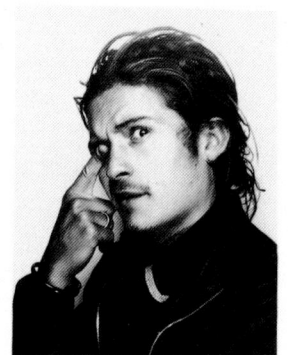

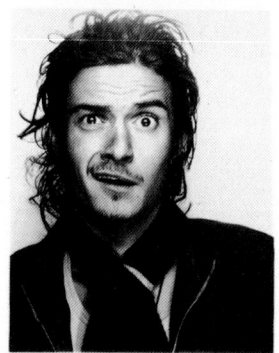

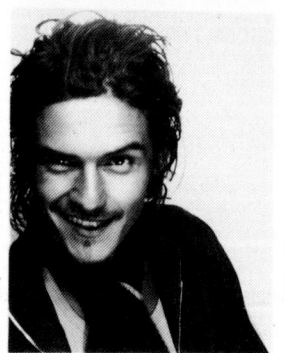

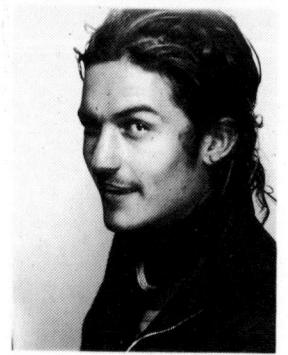

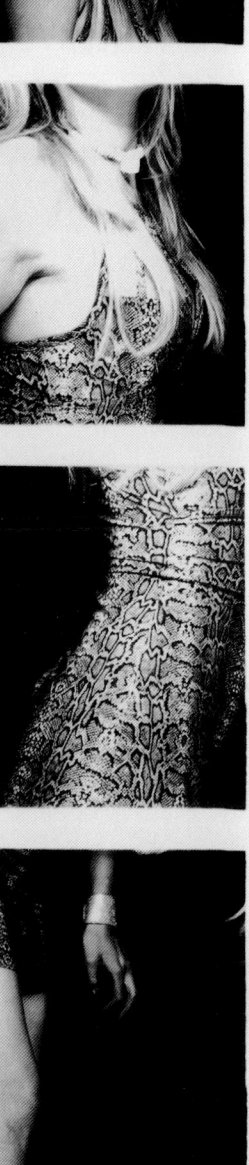

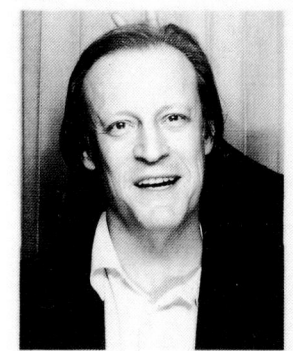
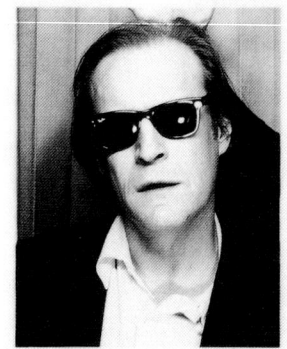
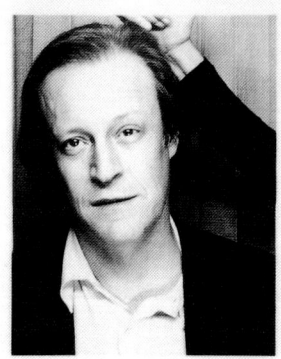
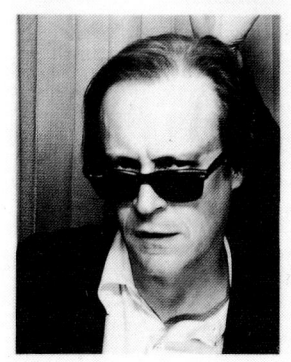

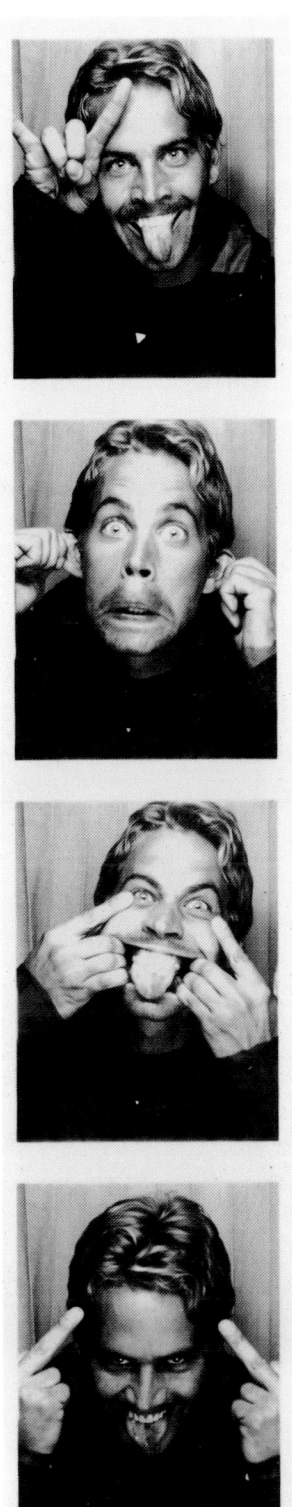

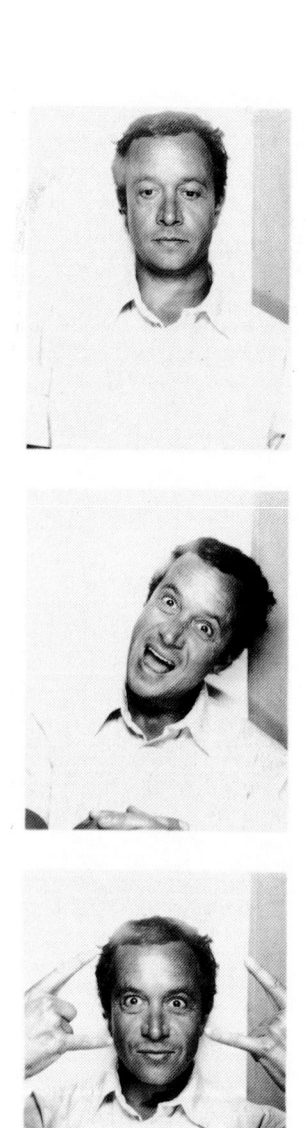
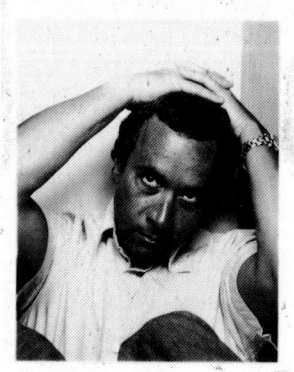

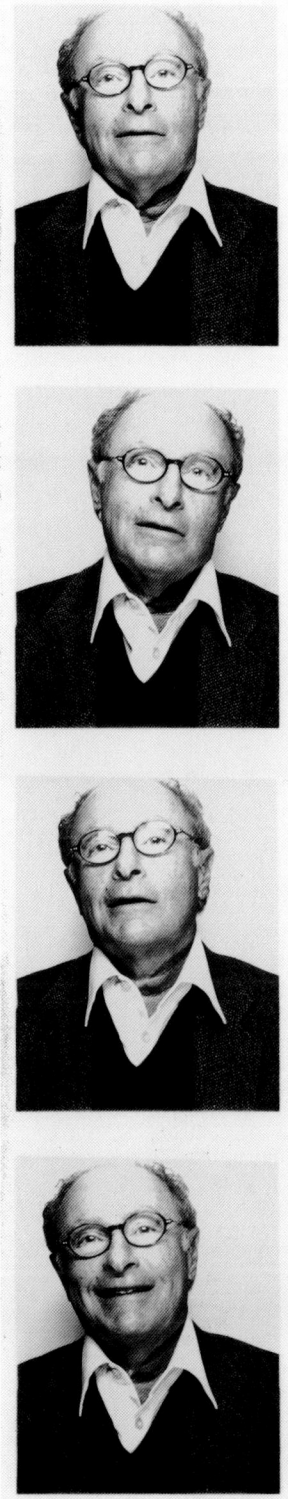

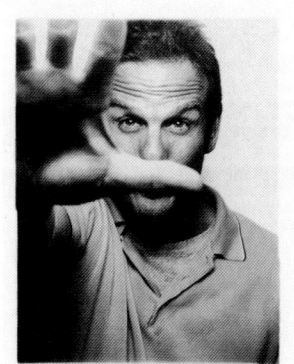

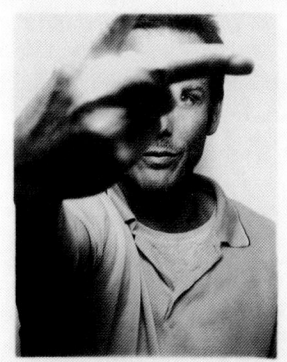

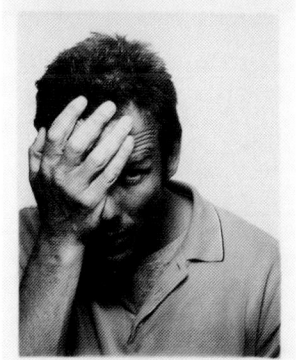

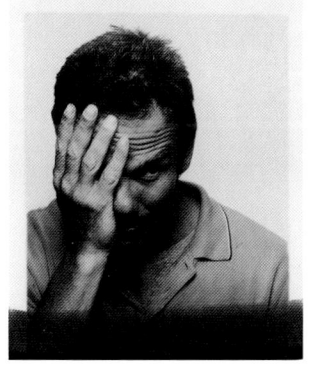

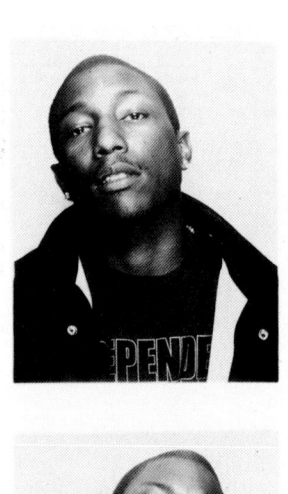

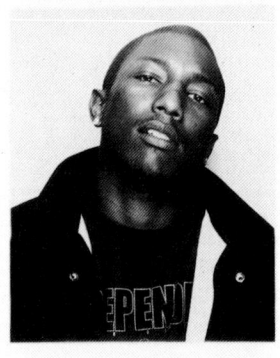

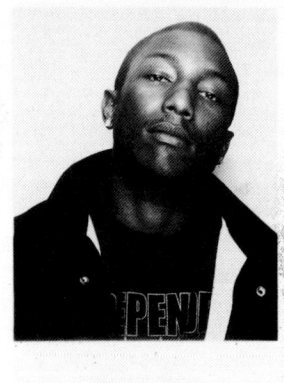

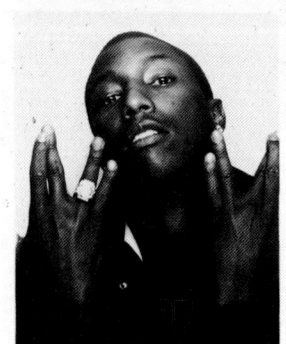

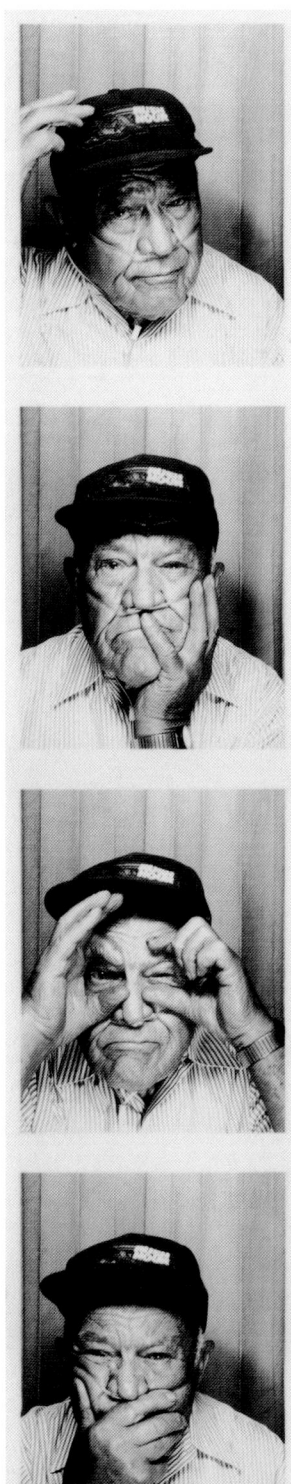

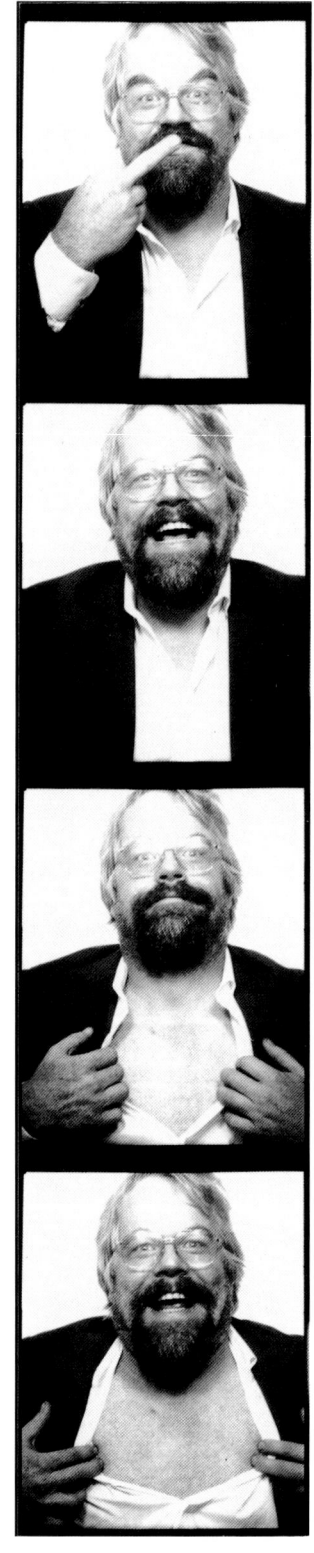

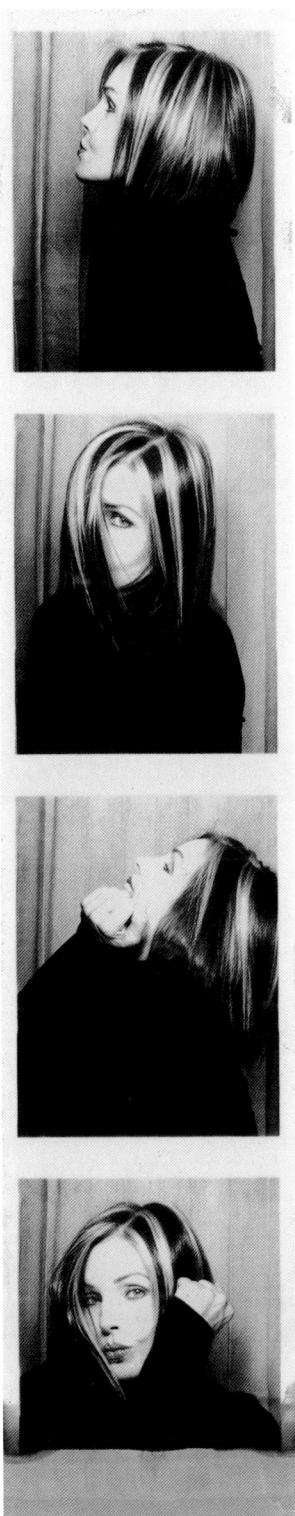

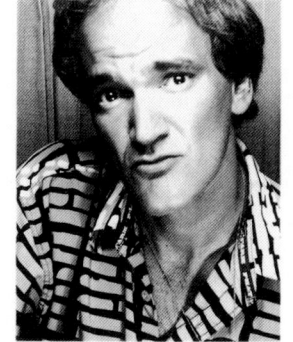
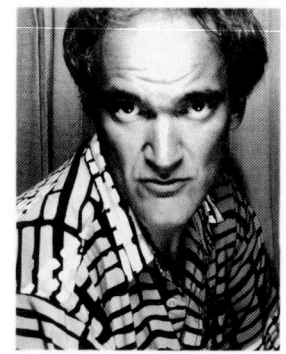
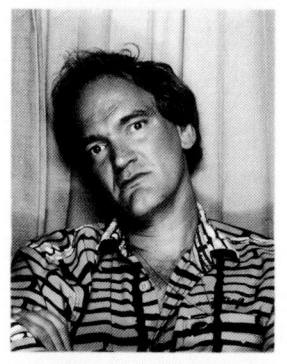
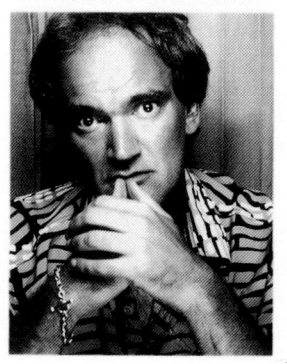

Quentin Tarantino

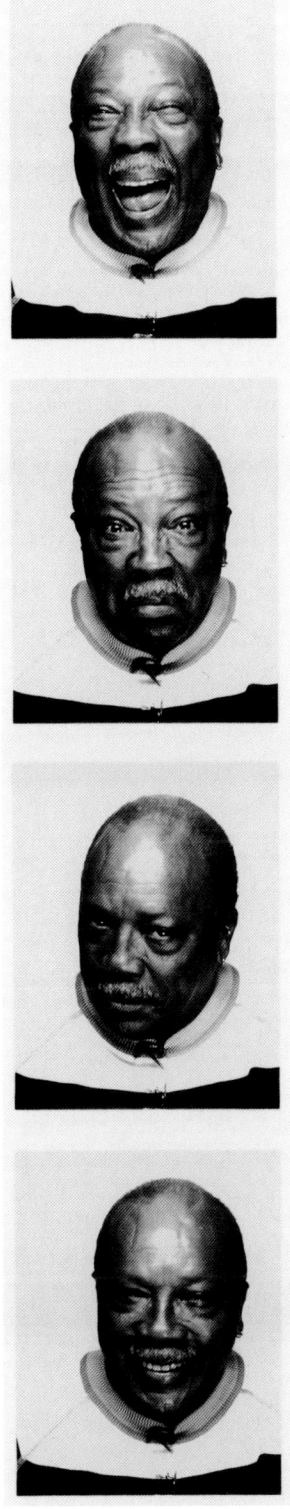

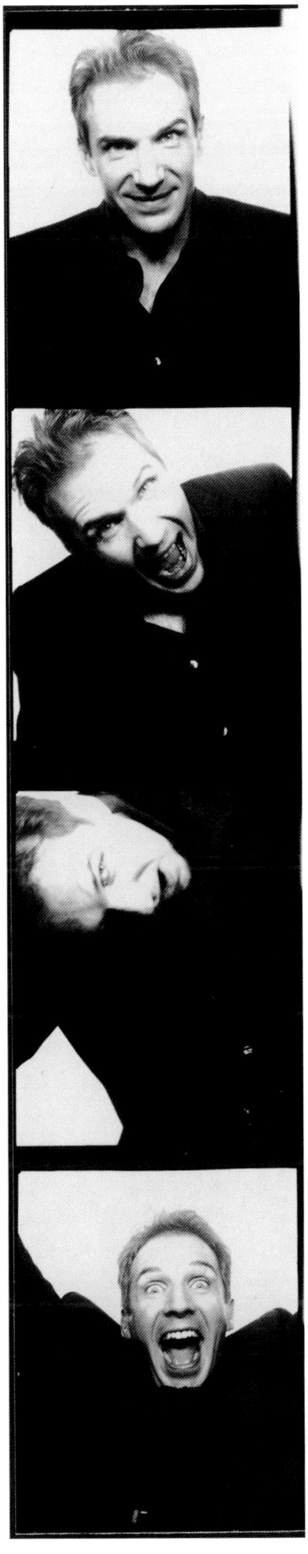

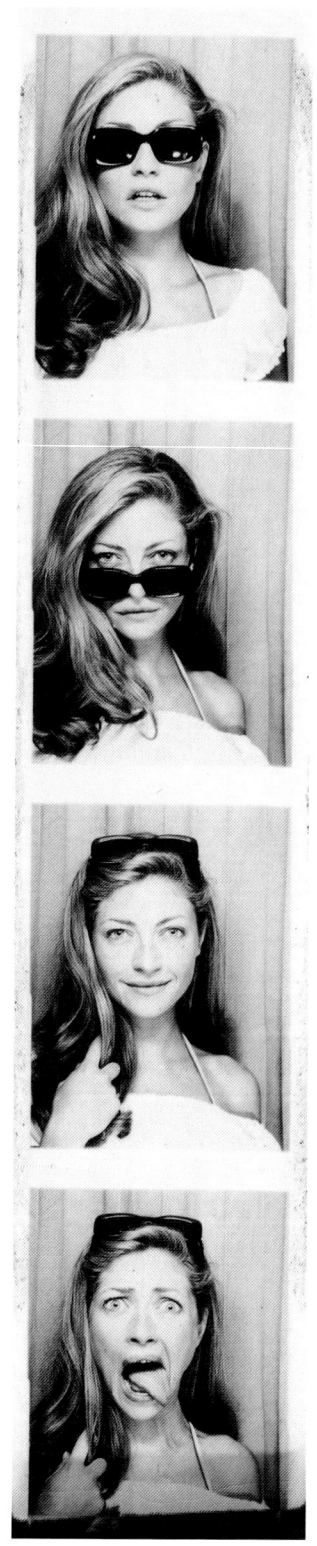

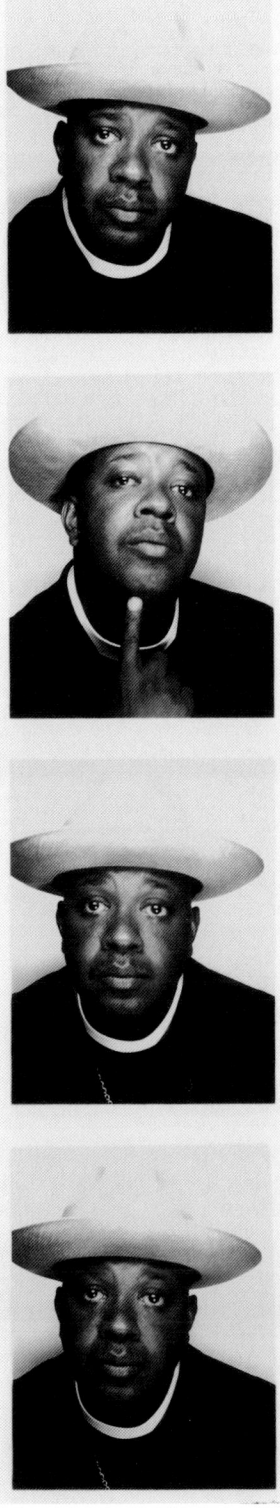

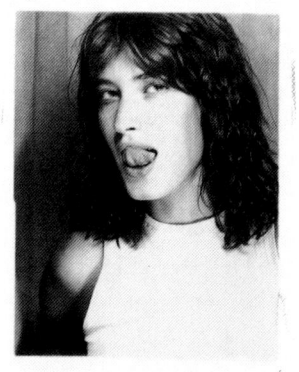

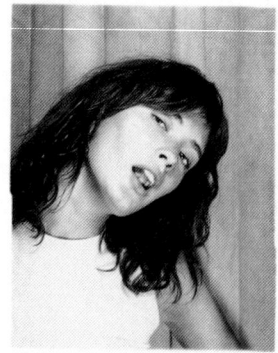

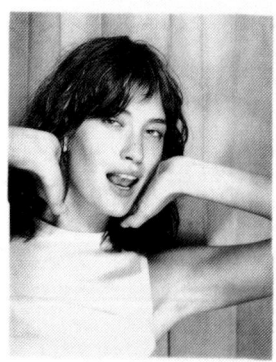

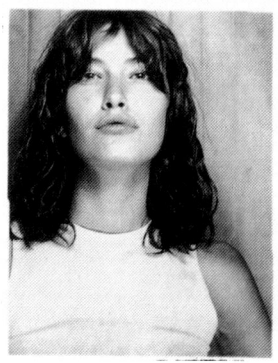

Rhea Durham

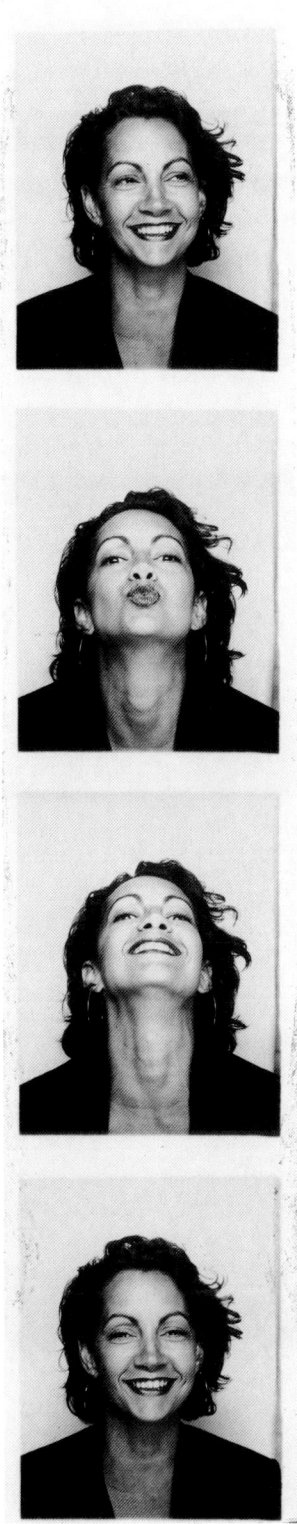

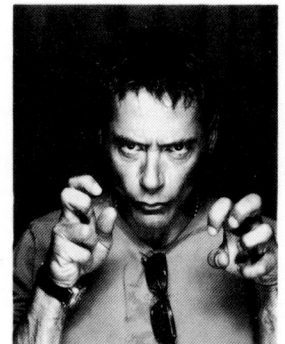

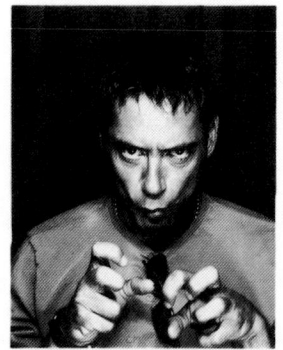

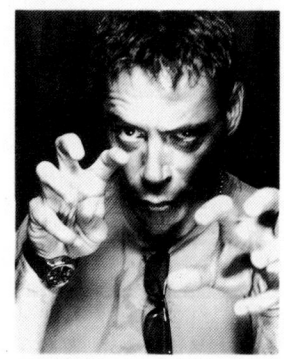

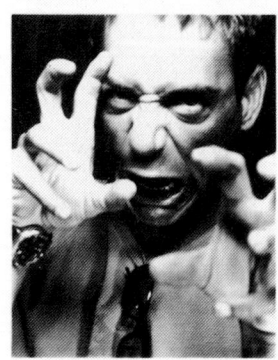

Robert Downey Jr.

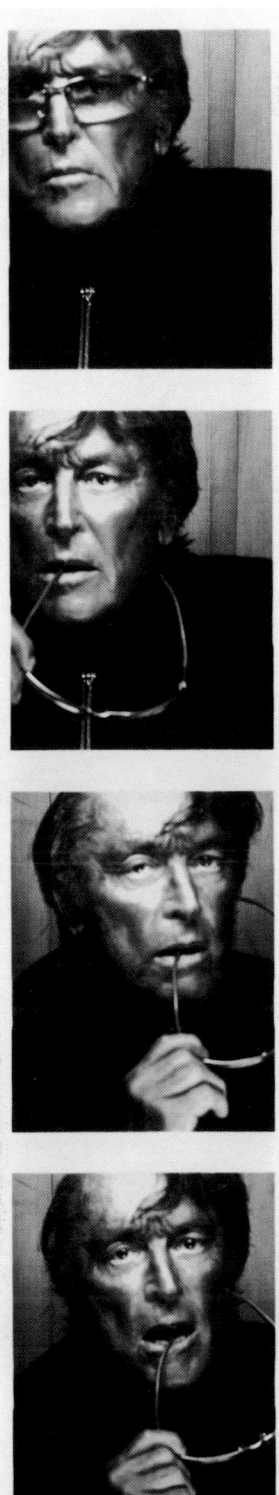

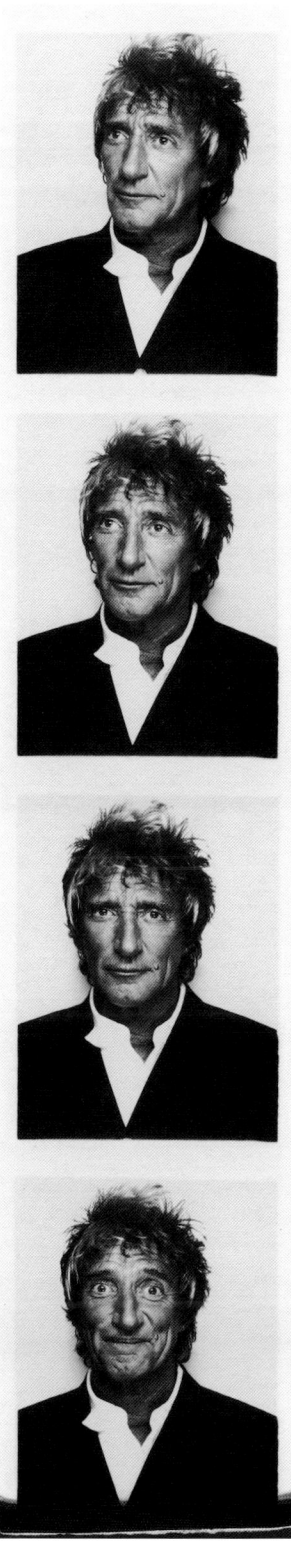

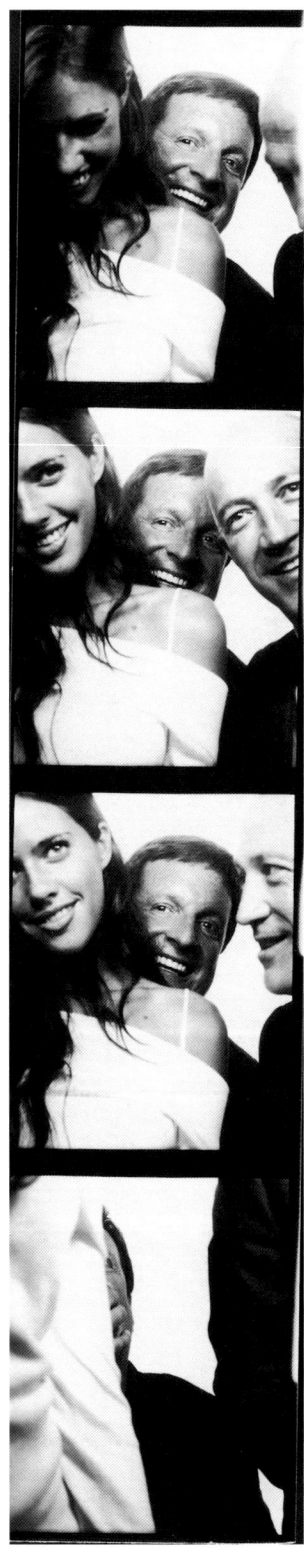

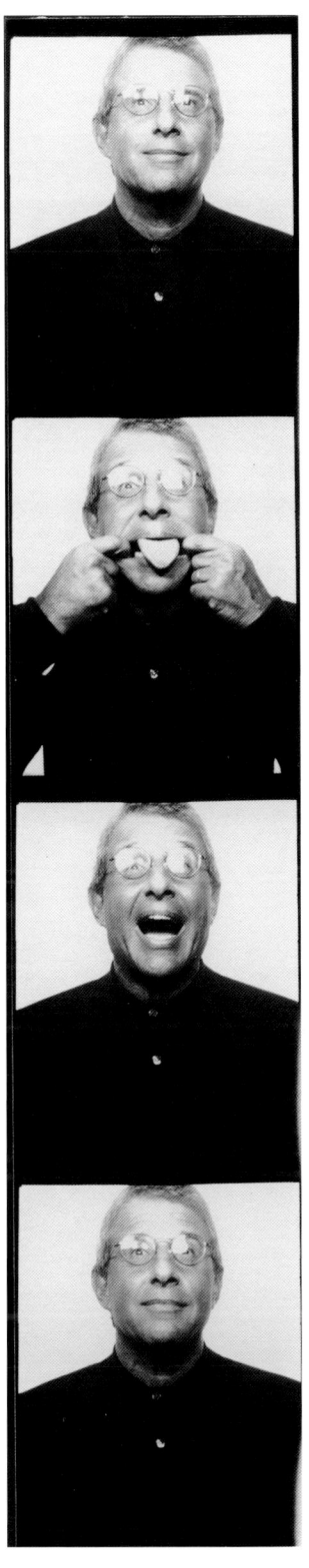

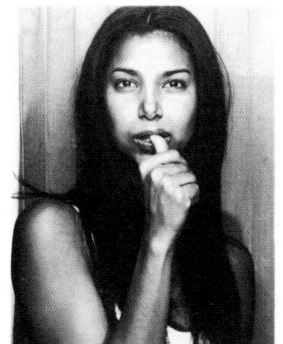
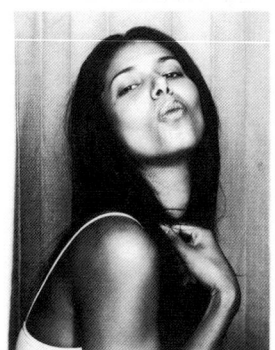
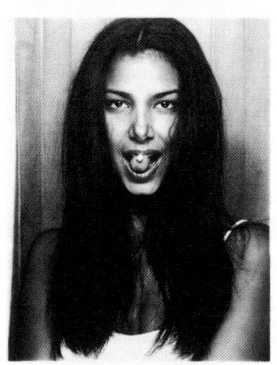
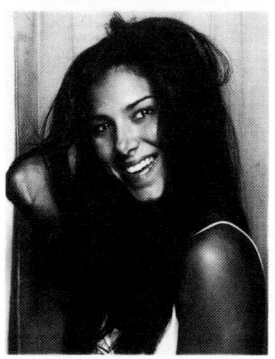

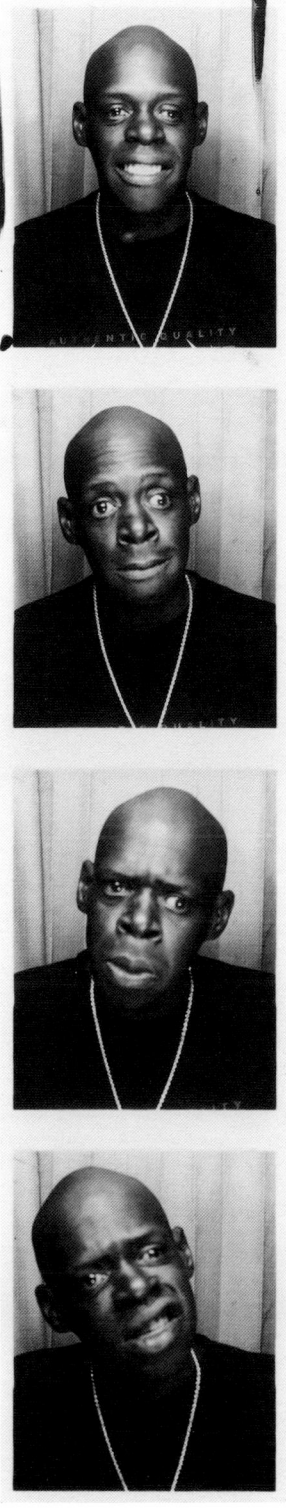

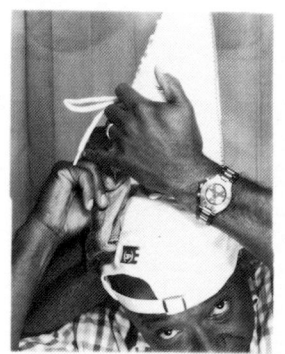

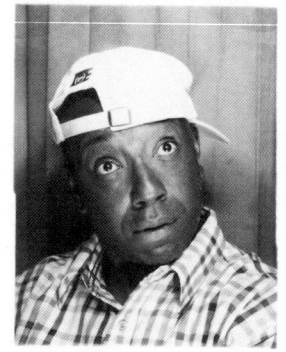

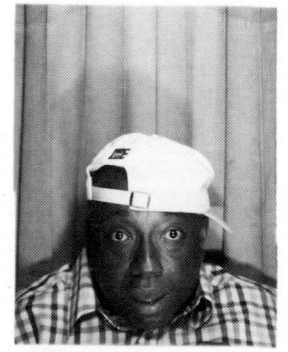

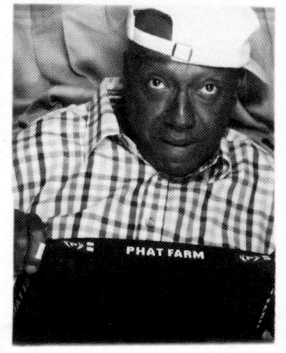

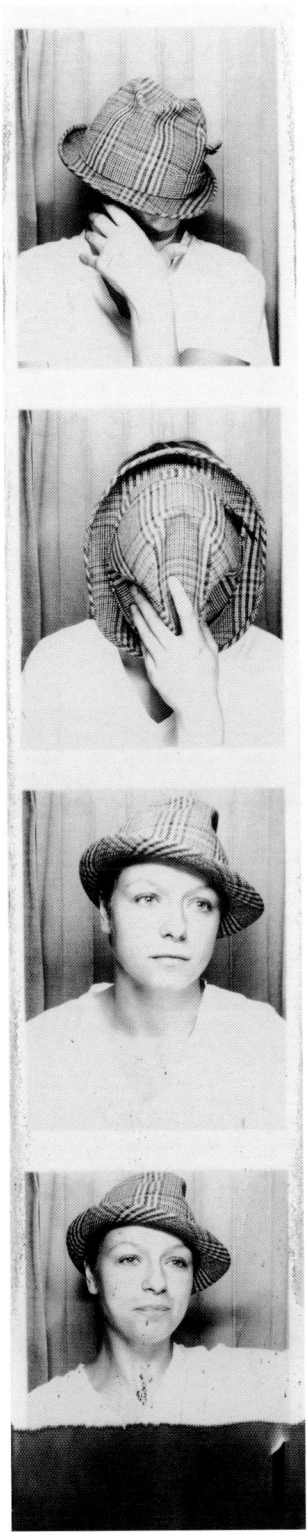

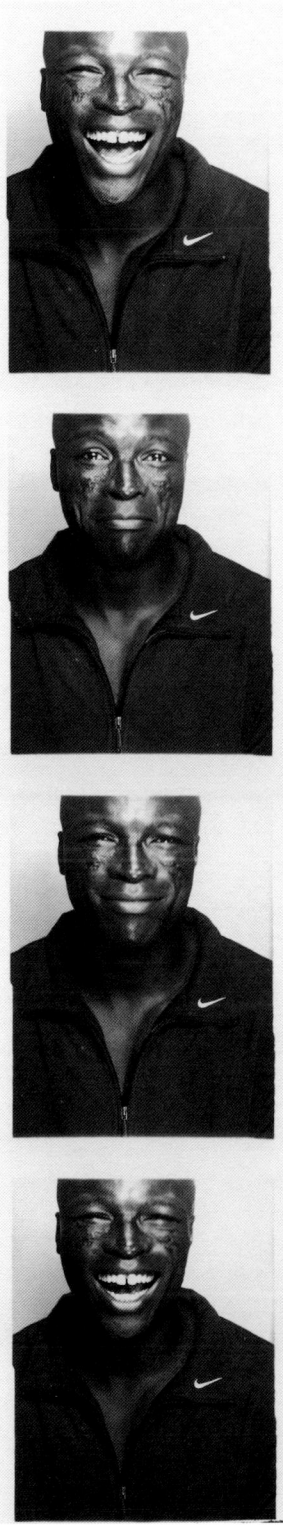

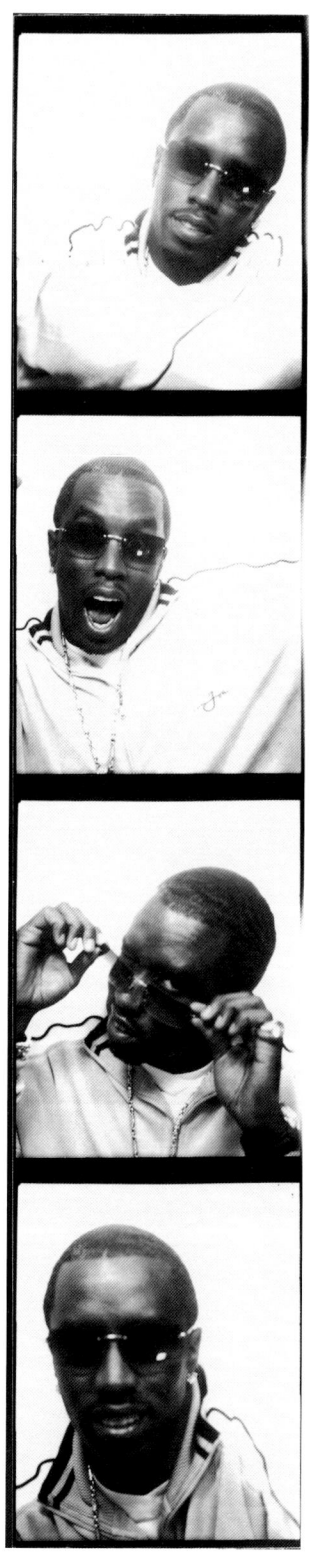

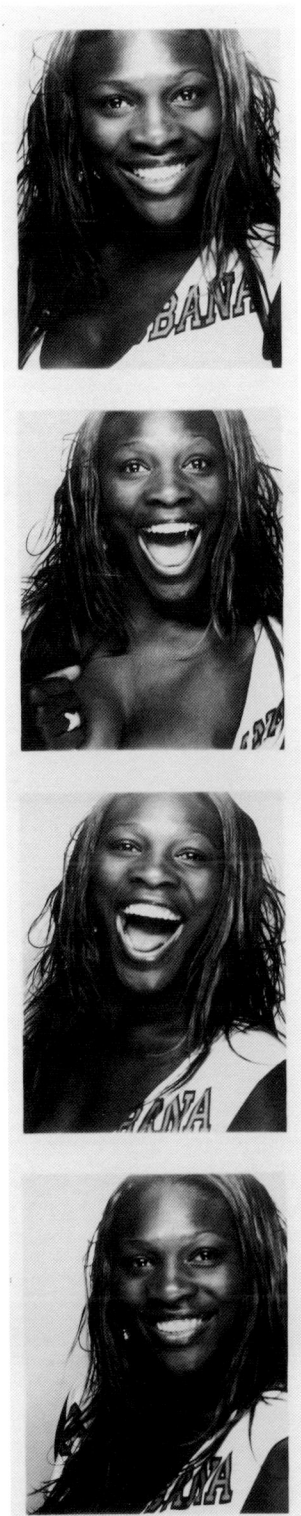

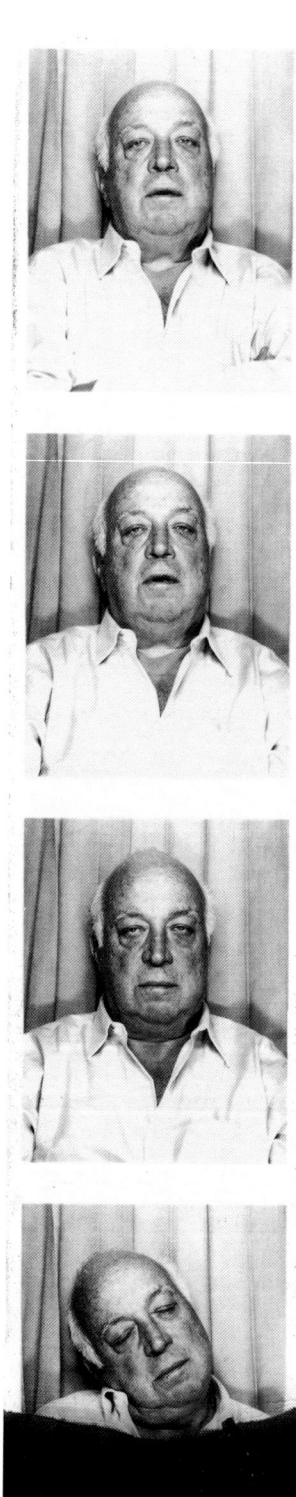

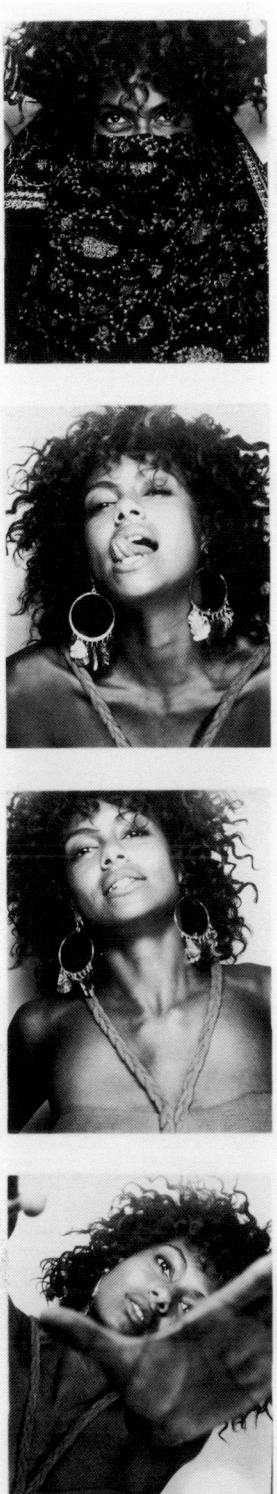

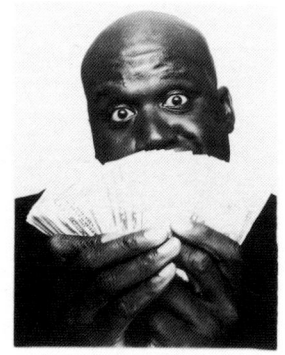
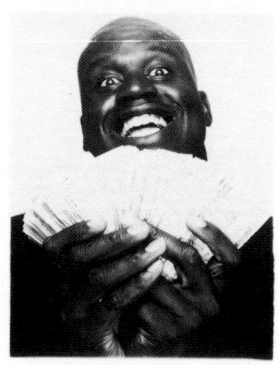
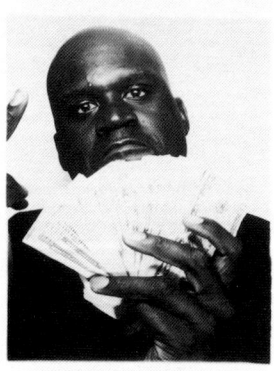
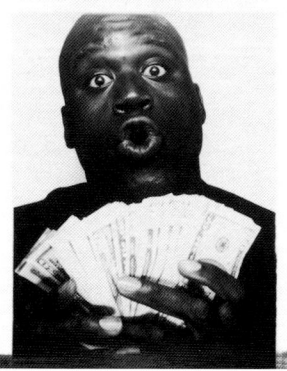

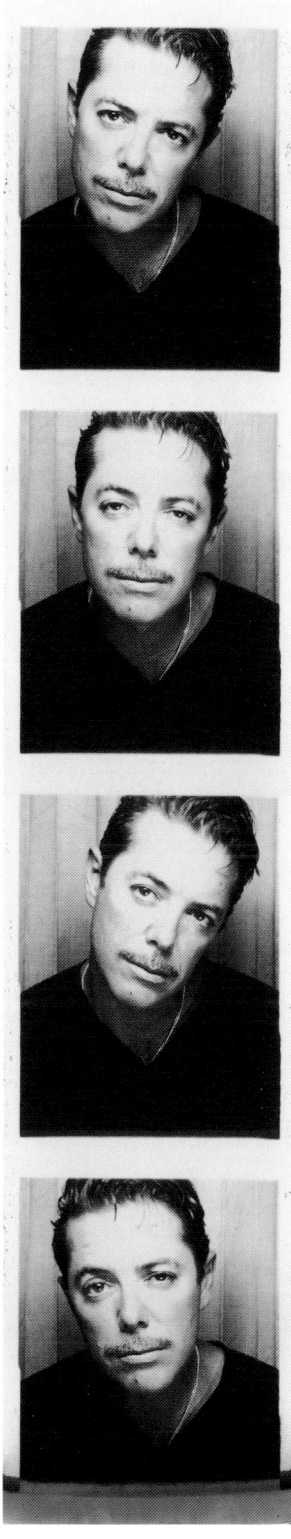

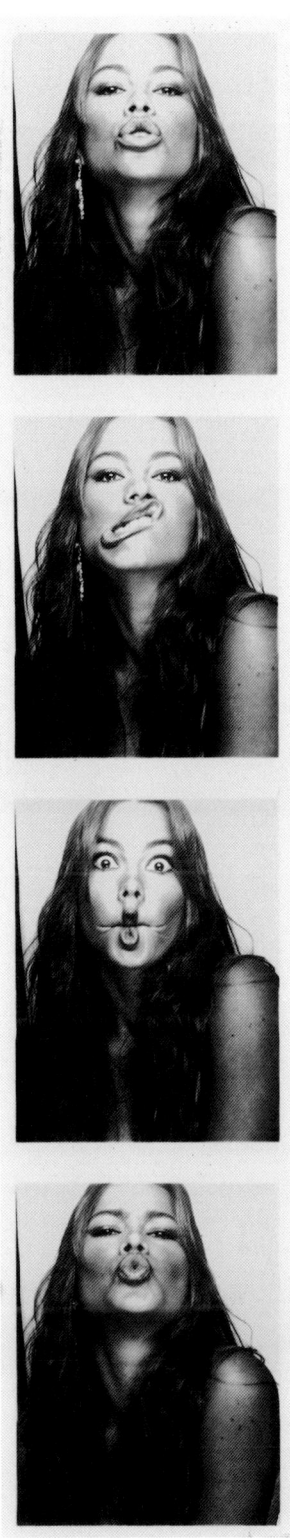

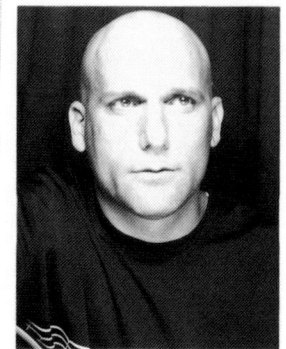
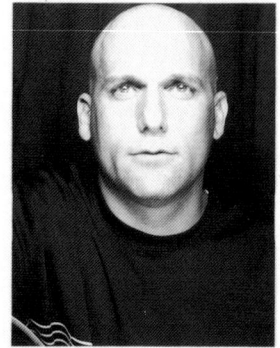
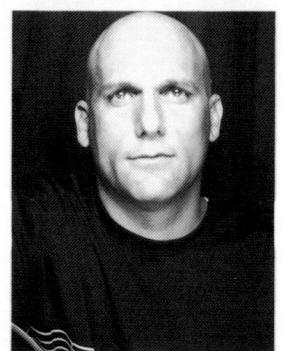
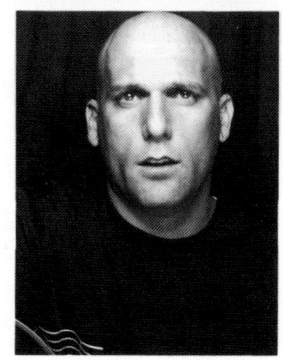

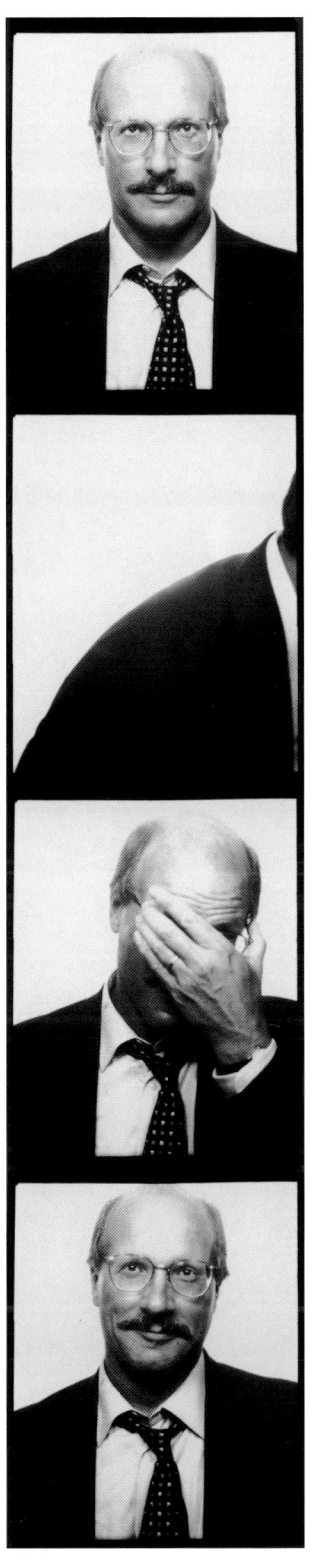

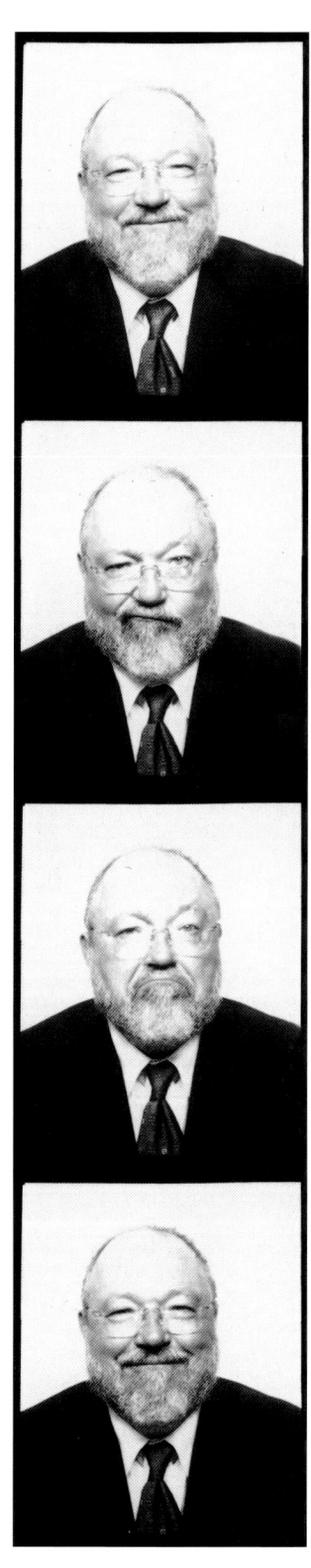

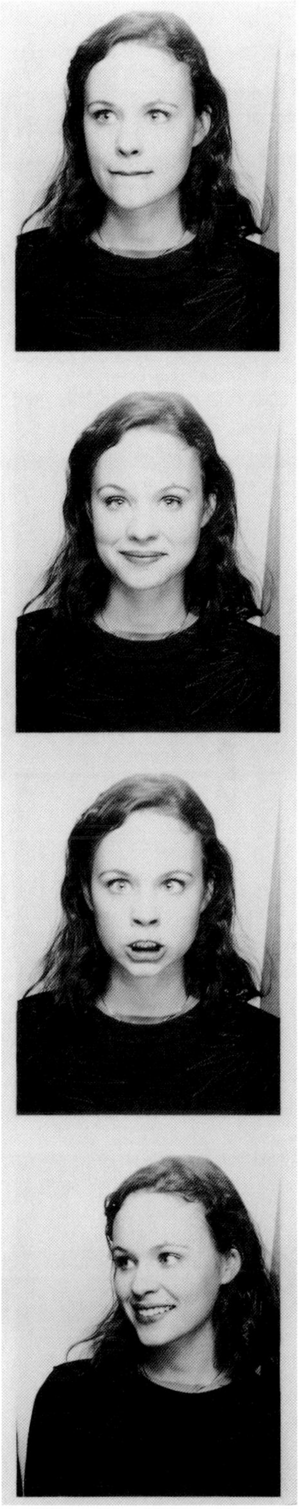

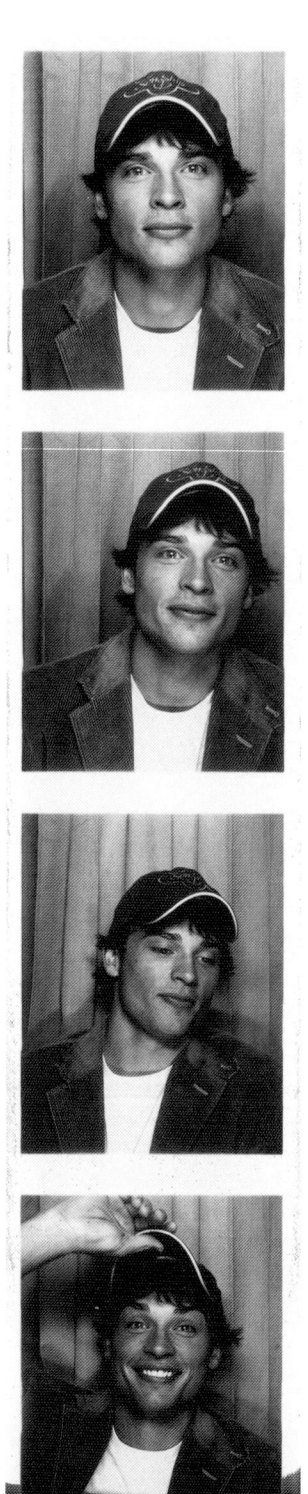

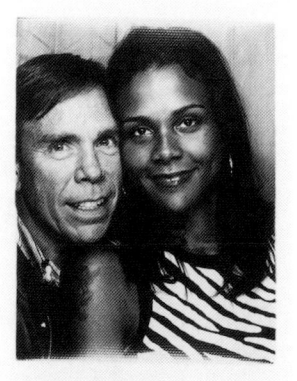
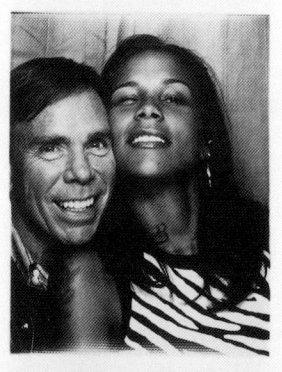
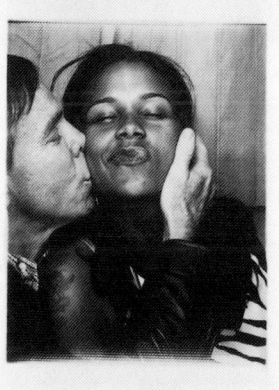
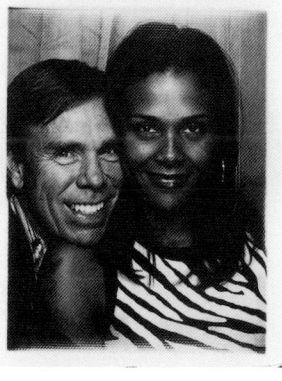

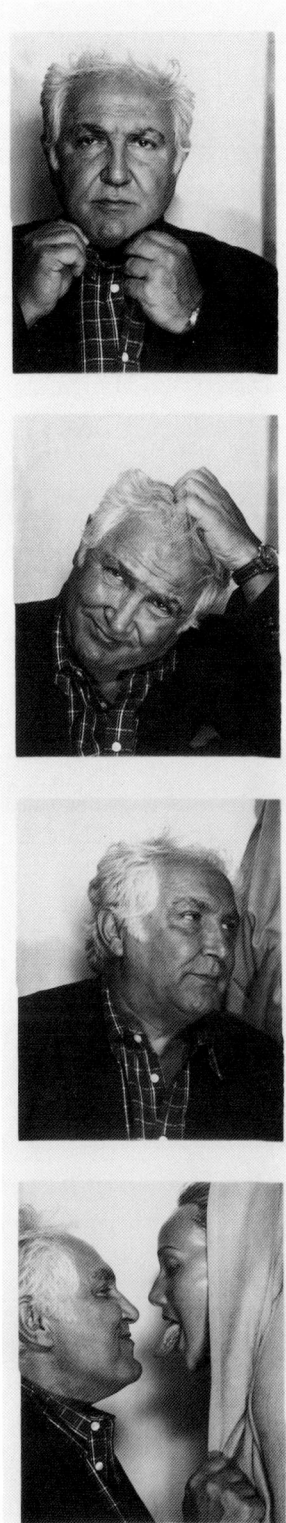

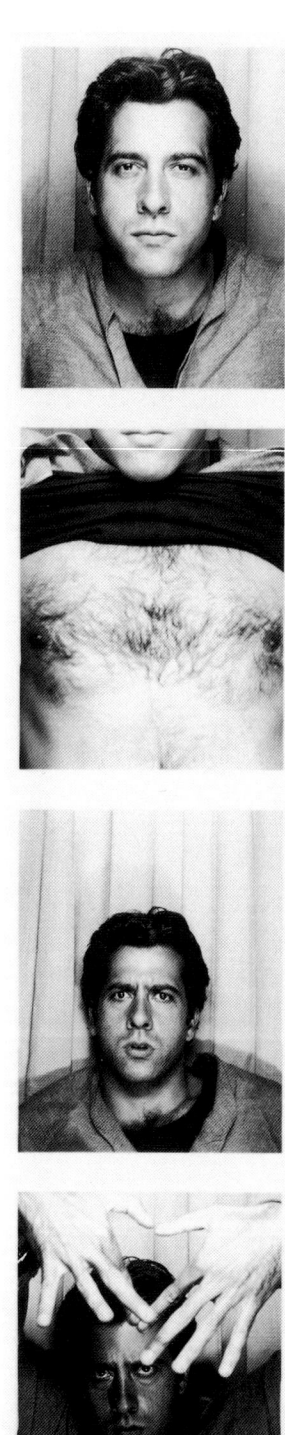

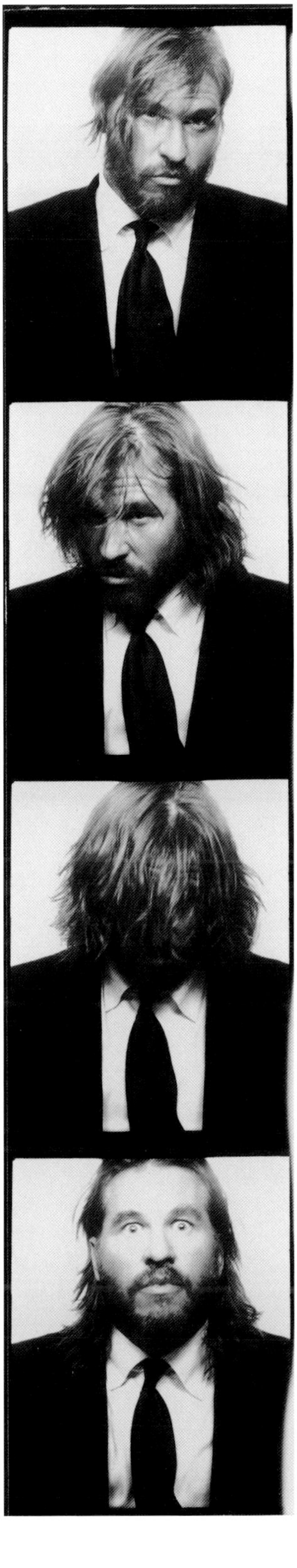

Val Kilmer

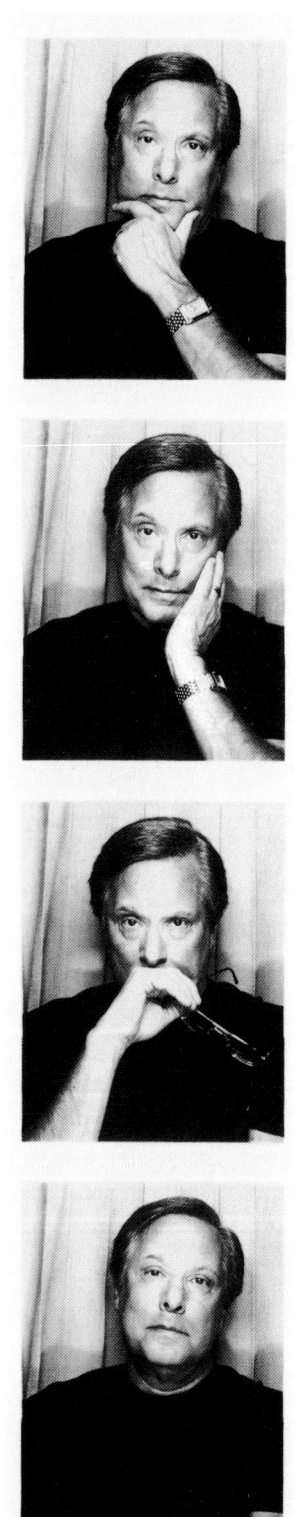

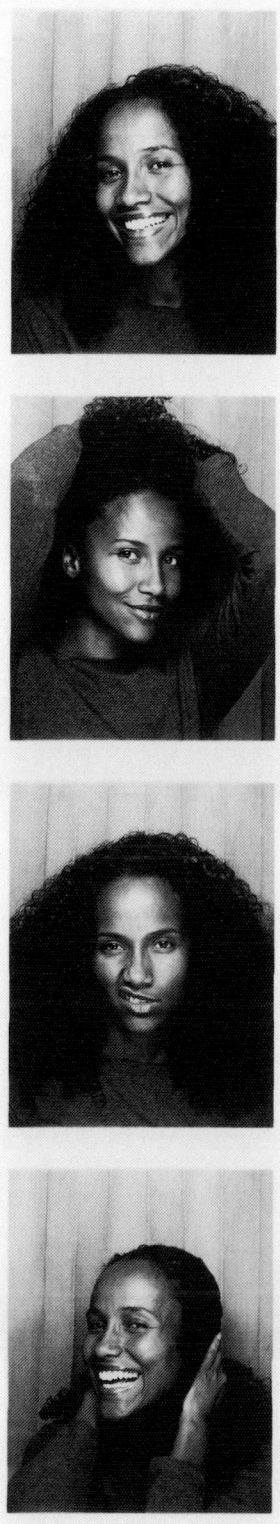

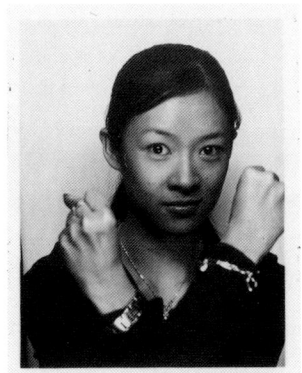
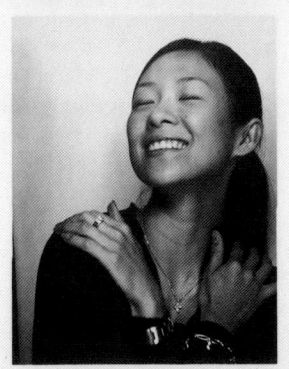
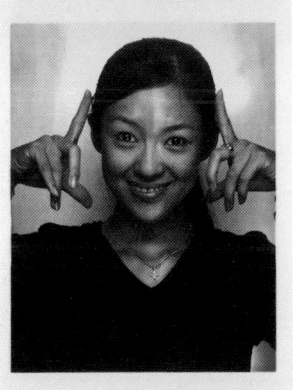
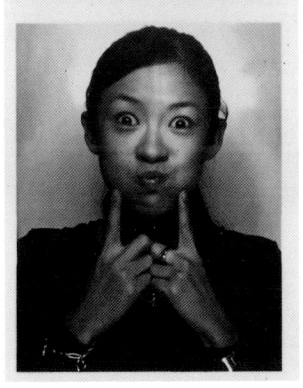

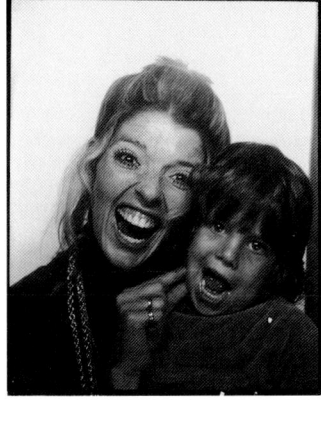

I would like to thank my Mom for all her love and guidance, and for sharing with me my first photo booth experience; my grandparents, Pipa and Fanita, for being supportive of everything I do; Rebecca Gayheart for her unconditional friendship and love; Alvin Malnik and Russell Simmons for mentoring me; Ally Bernstein who worked tirelessly on the book for months on end; Robert Evans for writing such a brilliant introduction and for continually inspiring me with his wisdom; Krista Smith for being the first to believe in the project, and for convincing Graydon Carter to publish an article on the book in the *Vanity Fair* "Hollywood Issue" before I even had a publisher; David Fahey for introducing me to powerHouse and helping me edit the book; Daniel Power, Meg Handler, and the staff at powerHouse Books for being so patient with all my last minute changes, and especially Heidi Thorsen for doing such a great job designing the book; Dave Mateovich for keeping the photo booth fully operational; my assistants, Anita S. Chang and David Steiman, for helping with all aspects of my life; Patrick Hanley for helping keep Hilhaven Lodge a beautiful place to live; my lawyers, Jake Bloom, Michael Schenkman, and Richard Thompson, for the legal work; Melissa Kates and Amanda Silverman of PMK for doing all the publicity; Geoff Katz, my new photo agent (I never thought I would have one); Glen E. Friedman for introducing me to the world of photography; Mark Helfrich for motivating me to publish photography books; Phil Stern for being my favorite photographer; and Michael Jackson for being such a good friend, and for constantly reminding me that it's okay to be a kid.

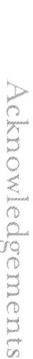

Acknowledgements

Robert Evans' lengthy career has touched every facet of the entertainment industry. He became the chief of worldwide production for Paramount Pictures at the age of thirty-six, when the company was nearing bankruptcy. Within four years, Evans raised Paramount from the eighth to the first position in the industry, and kept it there throughout his tenure. He held his position at Paramount for the longest period of time of any studio head since World War II. Under his auspices, Paramount produced such landmark hits as *Barefoot in the Park*, *Romeo and Juliet*, *Goodbye Columbus*, *The Longest Yard*, *Harold and Maude*, *Rosemary's Baby*, *Lady Sings the Blues*, *The Godfather*, and *The Godfather: Part II*.

Evans resigned from Paramount in 1975 to focus on producing, the year in which Paramount captured forty-three Academy Award nominations, a record unbroken to this day. He spent his first year purchasing novels and literary material for adaptation to film. After losing a bidding war over *The Valley of the Dolls* to 20th Century Fox, he was signed as an independent producer by Fox. His first acquisition was an unknown author's first novel, titled *The Detective*. The novel soon became a number one bestseller, and the film starred Frank Sinatra. Evans went on to produce such notable films as *Marathon Man*, *Urban Cowboy*, and *Sliver*.

Evans' career as an actor began at the age of eleven, when he became one of the most successful juvenile actors on radio, graduating into television when the medium was in its infancy. Later, Evans starred in such notable films as *The Sun Also Rises*, *The Best of Everything*, and *Man of a Thousand Faces* in which he played Irving Thalberg, the late producer who became the vice president of Metro-Goldwyn-Mayer at the age of twenty-five.

Evans is the only living producer to have two of his films singled out by the Library of Congress for preservation in perpetuity—*Chinatown* and *The Godfather*. He also holds the singular honor of having three of his films selected by the National Film Preservation Board to be included in the National Film Registry—*Chinatown*, *The Godfather*, and *The Godfather: Part II*. His autobiography, *The Kid Stays in the Picture*, is an international bestseller and has been made into a film. Robert Evans lives in Beverly Hills.

In a very short time, Brett Ratner has established himself as one of the most successful directors in Hollywood. At twenty-six years old he directed his first feature film, the 1997 surprise box office hit *Money Talks*, a comedy starring Charlie Sheen and Chris Tucker. His second film, the 1998 action comedy *Rush Hour*, starred Jackie Chan and Chris Tucker and earned $250 million worldwide. He followed that success with the romantic fantasy drama *The Family Man*, a critical and box office hit starring Nicolas Cage and Tea Leoni in 2000. A year later, Ratner delivered Hong Kong-style action with Chan and Tucker in the hit *Rush Hour 2*, which grossed more than $342 million worldwide. Ratner made his first foray into the world of suspense thrillers in 2002 with his fifth feature film *Red Dragon* starring Anthony Hopkins, Edward Norton, and Ralph Fiennes.

Raised in Miami Beach, Ratner had dreamed of being a filmmaker since the age of eight. He enrolled in New York University's Tisch School of the Arts at age sixteen, becoming the department's youngest film major. While attending NYU Film School, he made *Whatever Happened to Mason Reese*, a short film starring and about the former child actor. The award-winning project received funding from Steven Spielberg's Amblin Entertainment. Ratner's big break came after he screened his film for hip hop impresario Russell Simmons, launching a successful career in music videos. He has directed more than one hundred videos since then, for artists including Madonna, Mariah Carey, Jay-Z, Wu Tang Clan, D'Angelo, Heavy D, Mary J. Blige, Public Enemy, Sean "P. Diddy" Combs, and many others.

In 1999, Ratner won the MTV Award for Best Video for a Film for his video of Madonna's "Beautiful Stranger" from the *Austin Powers: The Spy Who Shagged Me* soundtrack. In addition, Ratner received a 2002 MTV Movie Award for Best Fight Sequence for *Rush Hour 2* as well as a 2003 TONY Award for producing Russell Simmons' Def Poetry Jam on Broadway. In 2001 Ratner was the recipient of the Spirit of Chrysalis Award for his leadership in helping economically disadvantaged and homeless individuals change their lives through employment opportunities. Brett Ratner lives in Beverly Hills.

A portion of the proceeds from the sale of this book will go to Brett Ratner's favorite charity—Chrysalis, a nonprofit organization dedicated to helping economically disadvantaged and homeless individuals become self-sufficient through employment opportunities. It currently helps more than two thousand individuals a year change their lives through jobs.

For more information about Chrysalis, visit their web site at www.changelives.org or call them at 310-392-4117. Thank you for helping bring hope and real opportunities to so many people.

HILHAVEN LODGE
The Photo Booth Pictures

© 2003 powerHouse Cultural Entertainment, Inc.
Photo Strips © 2003 Brett Ratner
Introduction © 2003 Robert Evans

Published in the United States by powerHouse Books,
a division of powerHouse Cultural Entertainment, Inc.
68 Charlton Street, New York, NY 10014-4601
telephone 212 604 9074, fax 212 366 5247
e-mail: photobooth@powerHouseBooks.com
web site: www.powerHouseBooks.com

First edition, 2003

Library of Congress Cataloging-in-Publication Data:

Ratner, Brett.
    Hilhaven Lodge : the photo booth pictures / photo strips by Brett Ratner ; introduction by
  Robert Evans.-- 1st ed.
      p. cm.
    ISBN 1-57687-195-9
    1. Celebrities--Portraits. 2. Photobooths. 3. Ratner, Brett--Homes and
  haunts--California--Los Angeles. I. Title.

  TR681.F3R363 2003
  779'.2'092--dc21

                                                    2003046707
Hardcover ISBN 1-57687-195-9

Scans by Gist, New Haven
Printing and binding by Artegrafica, Verona
Hilhaven Lodge: The Photo Booth Pictures is set in Mrs Eaves

Book design by Heidi Beatrice Thorsen

A complete catalog of powerHouse Books and Limited Editions is available upon request;
please call, write, or sit inside our web site.

10 9 8 7 6 5 4 3 2 1

Printed and bound in Italy